Standard Grade | General | Credit

English

First exam published in 2000.

Published by Leckie & Leckie, 8 Whitehill Terrace, St. Andrews, Scotland KY16 8RN tel: 01334 475656 fax: 01334 477392
enquiries@leckieandleckie.co.uk www.leckieandleckie.co.uk

Leckie & Leckie Project Team: Andrea Collington; Peter Dennis; Bruce Ryan

ISBN 1-84372-196-1

A CIP Catalogue record for this book is available from the British Library.

Printed in Scotland by Scotprint.

Leckie & Leckie is a division of Granada Learning Limited, part of ITV plc.

Acknowledgements

Leckie & Leckie is grateful to the copyright holders, as credited, for permission to use their material. Every effort has been made to trace the copyright holders and to obtain their permission for the use of copyright material. Leckie & Leckie will gladly receive information enabling them to rectify any error or omission in subsequent editions.

The Scotsman for a photograph (2001 General Reading paper p 2);

Polygon for the short story 'An Invisible Man' by Brian McCabe, originally published in *The Macallan/Scotland on Sunday collection of Short Stories* (2002 Credit Reading paper p 2):

Time Pix for a photograph by Jytte Bjerregaard (2002 Writing paper p 2);

Robert Doisneau & Maurice Baquet for a photograph (2002 Writing paper p 4);

The Royal Geographical Society for a photograph (2002 Writing paper p 8);

Faye Godwin for a photograph (2002 Writing paper p 10);

The Times, for an article by Catriona Marchant 'We're out for the Count' 13 October 2001 (2003 General Reading paper p 2);

Allstar Picture Library for a photograph (2003 Writing paper p 6);

The Mail on Sunday for the article 'Pucker way to kiss a hummingbird' by Mark Carwardine (2004 General Reading paper p 2);

Getty Images for a photograph (2004 Writing paper p 2);

Getty Images for a photograph (2004 Writing paper p 8);

Camera Press, London, for a photograph by John Swannell (2004 Writing paper p 10).

The following companies/individuals have very generously given permission to reproduce their copyright material free of charge:

Lesley Donald for a photograph (2000 General Reading paper p 2);

'Just when you thought it was safe to go back to North Queensferry' reproduced with the permission of *The Herald/Evening Times* (2000 General Reading paper p 2);

Extract from *Excursions In The Real World* by William Trevor published by Hutchinson. Used by permission of the Random House Group Limited (2000 Credit Reading paper p 2);

Catherine Czerkawska for an article from *The Scotsman* (2001 General Reading paper p 2);

Michael Munro for an extract from *Application* (2002 General Reading paper p 2);

FreeFoto.com for 4 photographs (2003 Writing paper pp 2, 4, 8 &10);

Extract from *Captain Corelli's Mandolin* by Louis de Berniéres. Reprinted by permission of The Random House Group Ltd. (2004 Credit Reading paper p2);

Maurice Lacroix Ltd for an advertisement (2004 Writing paper p 4);

News Team International for a photograph (2004 Writing paper p 6).

2000 GENERAL

G

0860/403

| NATIONAL QUALIFICATIONS 2000 | TUESDAY, 16 MAY 1.00 PM – 1.50 PM | ENGLISH STANDARD GRADE General Level Reading Text |

Read carefully the passage overleaf. It will help if you read it twice. When you have done so, answer the questions. Use the spaces provided in the Question/Answer booklet.

The following passage has been adapted from an article in "The Herald".

Just when you thought it was

Stephen McGinty

faces danger to swim with the sharks

1   There is a cartoon in the diver's locker room at Deep Sea World. It shows two sharks eyeing up a couple of divers in masks, fins and aqualungs. One shark asks the other, "Will we eat them?" The other replies, "No, that thing on their backs gives me wind."

2   As I bent, buckled and squeezed myself into the drysuit, the threat of a dose of marine indigestion seemed a poor defence against the flat-eyed terrors of the deep.

3   I had been assured at the North Queensferry complex that the sharks would have no wish to eat me. I did not look like their natural prey of fish, which are small, wet and flap about. No-one noticed that at the time I felt small, was drenched in sweat and couldn't stop shaking. I didn't feel like a flounder, but given time . . .

4   In the next chamber was the world's largest underwater safari: four and a half million litres of filtered sea water containing dozens of species and hundreds of fish including bass, cod, plaice, bream, mackerel, lesser spotted dogfish, conger eels, skates and sharks. The nine bigger sharks were sand tigers—the largest about nine feet long.

5   All the sand tigers have names like Stella, Bertha, Fred, Barnie and Dino. The largest is called The Preacher because most people see him and start to pray. Barnie sounded like a bundle of laughs in comparison.

6   "Mind, the big one is a bit frisky," said another diver to Stuart Bell, my scuba instructor.

7   "Frisky?" I nervously asked.

8   "Don't worry," Stuart said as he helped zip up my drysuit. To explain, a wet suit gets you wet; the water enters holes in the suit but doesn't exit, so your body-temperature heats the water, providing an insulating layer. A dry suit seals out the water allowing you to wear tracksuit bottoms and T-shirt underneath for warmth.

9   Once sealed inside our suits, we clambered into a tiny tank, containing only a few crabs, where I hauled on my aqualung and weight belt. Sinking to the bottom I struggled to gain my balance against the backwards pull of the weights and aqualung. Gripping Stuart's arm, I drained the air from the suit and accustomed myself to the sensation of breathing underwater.

10   When I was relaxed, Stuart opened the

Childhood fears are faced as a shark

hatch leading to the main safari tank. Rock walls dropped to the sandy floor 30 feet below.

11   Though the habitat felt natural, it would be impossible to view such a variety of sea-life in Scotland's brackish waters. Brightly coloured fish of greens, blues and greys darted, twisted and turned, and a giant skate flapped over the tunnel as tourists, wide-eyed in wonder, peered up as I looked down into an utterly silent world. The only sound was the rasp of my own breath and the click of swallowing.

12   Stuart descended first and I quickly followed squinting while the pressure built in my ears. Just as on an aeroplane, you can clear them by pinching your nose and blowing. On the bottom I lost balance but was supported by Stuart as I found my feet.

13   Childhood memories of underwater programmes on TV flooded in, mixing with books and magazines on sharks and the film cartoon of *Marine Boy*. Once I had gained some confidence, Stuart returned to the surface to collect underwater photographer Gavin Anderson. It was then I noticed the little four-year-old waving from the tunnel. I started to think: what if I was eaten by a nine-foot shark? Would it scar him for life? Then I put myself in his place. As a small child my only response to a diver being savaged to death by a giant shark just feet in front of me would be . . . COOOOOL!!!

safe to go to North Queensferry

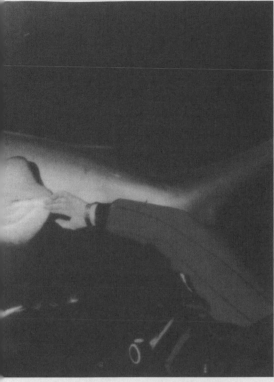

swims by, close enough to touch.

14   Deep Sea World was drawing them in with a blood-curdling exhibition about pirates. Just how much would the business boom if the sharks were to turn savage? It's all very well saying these sharks are environmentally friendly and only eat wee fish. That's boring; it's blood that the public want to see. I inched my head carefully, scanning for Stuart's return.

15   Panic and paranoia rose with my air bubbles as I caught a blurry glimpse of my foe curving around on the other side of the tunnel with a lazy flick of its tail. This sand tiger shark was nine feet long and approaching about six feet in front and above me. My lungs began to pipe the *Jaws* theme up in my throat.

16   A few images from the film looped in my head before it arrived: Robert Shaw desperately kicking at the munching mouth of the great white shark, before disappearing inside; the severed leg dropping to the bottom of the boating pond, a tumbling head, and Roy Schneider up on a sinking flag pole, taking aim and screaming, "Smile, you son of a . . . " BOOM!

17   And then it was before me in direct contrast to the celluloid nightmares of Hollywood. There was no evil eye staring me out, no prowling movement or even any interest. Instead it swam by like a bored fridge. Just then, water began to fill my mask obscuring the view. Once I had cleared it my foe-turned-

distant-friend was disappearing into the distance. Suddenly I felt a hand on my shoulder marking Stuart's return with photographer Gavin Anderson.

18   Gavin seemed confident and relaxed. "If we want to get a picture of you with a shark you're going to have to get quite close so I can blast it with the flash and get the shot."

19   "That won't annoy it?" I worried.

20   "What?"

21   "The shark, you won't annoy it?"

22   "It'll be fine," he said, shaking his head and administering a friendly pat.

23   Thirty feet down he fiddled with his camera while occasionally giving the OK signal—thumb and first finger in a circle while the remaining three stick up in the air. I responded, though the mouthpiece hid the manic grins I made.

24   To recap on the sunken scene, I was kneeling on the bottom with my tank to the tunnel. Stuart was stationed protectively to my left side while Gavin hung about on the right, itching to shoot. I felt like bad bait—only crowds of cod, bass and flounder flocked towards me.

25   Ten or twelve of them mobbed round my mask, occasionally touching the glass before fleeing. Then I remembered sharks eat fish and suddenly felt like jam in a swiss roll at a kids' tea party. But they wouldn't leave. Just then Gavin got excited which could mean only one thing— the return of the floating fridge.

26   Earlier, while changing, we had rehearsed how I would tilt my head backwards so that my face and the shark's would fit inside the same picture. But I couldn't do it. I didn't want to. I slightly tilted my head and noticed the soft underbelly breeze above me, close enough to touch. This was real, not an image from a movie.

27   The finest moment of a memorable dive was when we slowly rose to the surface as a giant skate flapped past on one side while a sand tiger shark browsed by below me. The chance of such an encounter in the open seas would be as slim as my chances of survival without Stuart's reassuring presence and training.

28   Breaking the surface and wrenching out the mouthpiece, I swore, and swore, and swore. Swearing is sometimes more descriptive for the indescribable as the words come charged with more impact. I had swum with sharks. Childhood fears and attractions had been relived when I touched another world. I simply wanted to return.

[END OF PASSAGE]

[BLANK PAGE]

G

Total
Mark

0860/404

NATIONAL
QUALIFICATIONS
2000

TUESDAY, 16 MAY
1.00 PM – 1.50 PM

ENGLISH
STANDARD GRADE
General Level
Reading
Questions

Fill in these boxes and read what is printed below.

Full name of centre

Town

Forename(s)

Surname

Date of birth
Day Month Year

Scottish candidate number

Number of seat

**NB Before leaving the examination room you must give this booklet to the invigilator.
If you do not, you may lose all the marks for this paper.**

SCOTTISH
QUALIFICATIONS
AUTHORITY

©

QUESTIONS

Write your answers in the spaces provided.

Look at Paragraphs 1 to 3.

1. **Write down** an expression the writer uses which suggests that he was having difficulty getting dressed for diving.

    _____

    2
    0

2. **Write down** an expression he uses to show how he feels about the sharks.

    _____

    2
    0

3. (*a*) What reason was the writer given for believing that the sharks wouldn't want to eat him?

    _____

    2
    0

    (*b*) Explain fully why the writer was not reassured by this reason.

    _____

    _____

    _____

    2
    1
    0

4. "I didn't feel like a flounder, but given time . . . "
    Why do you think the writer **deliberately** chose not to complete this sentence?

    _____

    _____

    2
    1
    0

Look at Paragraphs 4 and 5.

5. "In the next chamber was the world's largest underwater safari . . ."
    Show how the writer continues this idea throughout Paragraph 4.

    _____

    _____

    2
    1
    0

6. Explain fully how The Preacher got its name.

_____

_____

2
1
0

Look at Paragraphs 6 to 9.

7. Explain the difference between a wet suit and a dry suit by completing the following sentences. **Use your own words as far as possible.**

   (i) A wet suit keeps you warm by _____

_____

_____

2
1
0

   (ii) A dry suit keeps you warm by _____

_____

_____

2
1
0

8. Explain clearly why the writer had to struggle to keep his balance at the bottom of the small tank.

_____

_____

2
1
0

Look at Paragraphs 10 to 12.

9. Once he was in the main safari tank, the writer noticed various aspects of the fish and their world. Give **three** of them.

   (i) _____

   (ii) _____

   (iii) _____

2
1
0

10. Apart from the loss of balance, what other problem did the writer experience, and how did he overcome it?

_____

_____

2
1
0

Look at Paragraphs 13 and 14.

11. Why do you think the writer has chosen the word "flooded" to describe how his memories returned?

_____

_____

2
1
0

12. The writer notices a little four-year-old watching him.

(*a*) Explain clearly why the writer worried about this at first.

_____

_____

2
1
0

(*b*) Why did he change his mind?

_____

_____

2
1
0

13. ". . . it's blood that the public want to see." (Paragraph 14)

What evidence does the writer give that savagery is good for business at Deep Sea World?

_____

_____

2
1
0

Look at Paragraphs 15 to 22.

14. What effects did the "blurry glimpse" (Paragraph 15) of the shark have on the writer?

_____

_____

2
1
0

15. ". . . it swam by like a bored fridge." (Paragraph 17)

Explain how effective you find this comparison.

_____

_____

2
1
0

16. **Write down** an expression from this section which shows that the writer's attitude towards the shark had started to change.

_____

17. Explain clearly what worried the writer about having his picture taken with a shark.

_____

_____

Look at Paragraphs 23 to 26.

18. What expression tells us that the writer was still worried even though he responded to the photographer's OK signal?

_____

19. **In your own words**, explain clearly why the writer felt "like jam in a swiss roll at a kids' tea party". (Paragraph 25)

_____

_____

Look at Paragraphs 27 and 28.

20. Explain fully why the writer felt that the finest moment was "when we slowly rose to the surface". (Paragraph 27)

_____

_____

21. **In your own words**, explain why the writer thinks that swearing can sometimes be more effective than using ordinary words.

_____

_____

[Turn over for Question 22 on *Page six*

Think about the passage as a whole.

22. "I had swum with sharks." (Paragraph 28)

   (*a*) What evidence is there earlier in the article that he had had a childhood interest in sharks?

   _____

   _____

   (*b*) From your reading of the article, how do you think the writer felt about sharks or his experience of swimming with them **compared with his expectations**?

   _____

   _____

   _____

[END OF QUESTION PAPER]

G

0860/403

NATIONAL
QUALIFICATIONS
2001

MONDAY, 14 MAY
1.00 PM – 1.50 PM

ENGLISH
STANDARD GRADE
General Level
Reading
Text

Read carefully the passage overleaf. It will help if you read it twice. When you have done so, answer the questions. Use the spaces provided in the Question/Answer booklet.

The Appeal of

1   All the junk in Scotland meets your befuddled gaze: thousands of unwanted gifts, the "wee something" for Christmas and the "I saw this and thought of you" for your birthday (how you wish they hadn't); then there are the holiday souvenirs. In short, all the stuff with which we tend to clutter our lives and our cupboards has somehow ended up in one place, awkwardly arranged on a vast number of folding tables.

2   Behind them, all kinds of people are perched on the tailgates of a variety of vehicles. Is this some bizarre store for recycled rubbish? Well, in a way it is. In other words, you have found yourself in the middle of your first car boot sale. They can be found most weekends in summer, and sometimes in winter too, in villages, towns and cities throughout the country. Sometimes they are held on an occasional basis—a charity or other organisation will hire a hall or a school playground, advertise in the local press and rent out pitches at £5 or £10 for the day. Other sales are held every Saturday or Sunday on more permanent sites.

3   Women seem to outnumber men behind the essential tables: although men often come to help to set up, they retire shyly for most of the day and return in the late afternoon to pack up the left-overs. Curiously enough, there are as many male customers as female: all human life wanders by.

4   There goes a plump medallion man who will tell you—his unhappily captive audience—a succession of unfunny and wildly politically incorrect jokes at which you will laugh, lamely, and hope he goes away.

5   There goes a succession of polite elderly gentlemen, clean and smart in their car coats; they will go off happily clutching boxes of your ancient gardening tools to which their wives will most surely object, but who are you to spoil their fun?

6   There is, just occasionally, a serious side to all this, which may affect the buyer rather than the genuine seller. Car boot sales can provide a certain amount of cover for less honest traders and it is as well to bear this in mind if you are offered a more than average bargain. Where, for instance, did those big canisters of cleaning fluid designated "Janitorial Supplies" originate? And what about those suspiciously home-made looking video cassettes of all the latest movies? Trading Standards Officers sometimes visit boot sales to keep a lookout for fakes. Police

Never underestimate what will sell. Old console games or market for all

occasionally find stolen goods lurking among the junk. Customs and Excise may be investigating those suspiciously cheap cigarettes and Environmental Health Officers may even be wondering whether that delicious home-made tablet has been concocted with due regard to public health.

7   But on the whole, say the police, they have little trouble with car boot sales. Most are legitimate and harmless: ordinary punters offloading bric-a-brac onto other ordinary punters. To a Martian hovering up there we must all look like nothing so much as a colony of ants, struggling to carry off various large and cumbersome objects, a table here, a suitcase there . . .

8   So if you fancy trying a boot sale, just for the fun of it, here are a few ground rules for participating in this most rewarding game.

9   Go as a buyer first, if you can. Have a good look around. Some pitches are better than others. Some are closer to the loos. Some are on windy corners and some may be right next to the little roundabout that plays the same four-bar tune all day long.

10 Go early, if you are selling. Many car boot sales that advertise an opening time of 10 am are being set up by seven or eight in the morning.

Car Boot Sales

videos will disappear as if by magic and there is a ready kinds of gadgets.

11   Beware of the antique dealers. They will surround your table at this early hour like wild dogs around a carcase, fingering your Aunty Annie's floral teapot with its dripping spout and trying to decide if they are getting the bargain of the century at £1·50 including chipped lid. Remember the Antiques Roadshow. Remember that daft little pottery owl that fetched thousands.

12   Invest in a cheap wallpapering table. You can sell out of the boot of your car, but if you have as much junk to get rid of as most of us do, you will need more space than the average hatchback can supply. Take a secure container for your money—preferably a money belt so that you can keep your takings safely about your person. Don't leave handbags lying around; car boot sales are hunting grounds for purse snatchers. By the same token it's wise to take a friend. Then you have someone to mind the stall while you take time out to browse around the neighbouring stalls.

13   Don't sell old electrical goods: they can be dangerous, and you can be in trouble with the law for doing so.

14   Take lots of food and drink with you: sandwiches, chocolate bars, flasks of tea and coffee, cans of soft drinks. You will be amazed at how hungry and thirsty you will get standing around all day and there is little point in blowing your takings on hamburgers although the smell will certainly drive you wild. Wear comfortable shoes and remember to take warm clothes, even in summer. Remember to plan for rain. This is Scotland after all, and you will probably get cold and wet.

15   Don't overprice your goods, but never underestimate what will sell either. The truth is that people will buy almost anything if the price is right. Old Playstation games, or genuine second-hand videos, will disappear as if by magic. Even more surprisingly, so will large, rickety (and empty) wooden boxes, elderly baseball caps that were given free with something ten years ago, shabby plastic dinosaurs that have been in many an imaginary battle and a pile of kitchen gadgets such as the tattie peeling machine that always took ages to wash afterwards, the expensive plastic containers with ill-fitting lids and the pancake mixer that liberally sprinkled you with batter every time you tried to use it. Just lay it out and somebody will come along wanting to buy it.

16   Above all, don't expect to make any fortunes. What you will do is recycle a truly astonishing amount of junk, give an amazing amount of pleasure to all kinds of people, observe all human life wandering past your table, and come home with a modest profit. That's if you can stop yourself from filling your car boot with other people's junk before you go home.

17   After all there's a little collection of pressed glass over there that is so irresistible, and the old hand-knitted Shetland shawl that nobody seems to have spotted, and isn't that a genuine stone hot-water bottle lurking among the rubbish . . . ?

Adapted from an article in "The Scotsman" by Catherine Czerkawska.

[END OF PASSAGE]

[BLANK PAGE]

FOR OFFICIAL USE

G

Total
Mark

0860/404

NATIONAL
QUALIFICATIONS
2001

MONDAY, 14 MAY
1.00 PM – 1.50 PM

ENGLISH
STANDARD GRADE
General Level
Reading
Questions

Fill in these boxes and read what is printed below.

Full name of centre

Town

Forename(s)

Surname

Date of birth
Day Month Year   Scottish candidate number   Number of seat

**NB Before leaving the examination room you must give this booklet to the invigilator.
If you do not, you may lose all the marks for this paper.**

SCOTTISH
QUALIFICATIONS
AUTHORITY

MCB   0860/404   6/71520

©

QUESTIONS

Write your answers in the spaces provided.

Look at Paragraphs 1 and 2.

1. "All the junk in Scotland meets your befuddled gaze"

   How does the writer continue the idea of "junk" in the first two paragraphs?

   _____

   _____

   2
   1
   0

2. **Write down an expression** from Paragraph 2 which shows that the writer thinks this "junk" makes a **strange collection**.

   _____

   2
   1
   0

3. Explain the **differences** between the two types of car boot sale described in Paragraph 2.

   (i) _____

   _____

   2
   1
   0

   (ii) _____

   _____

   2
   1
   0

Look at Paragraphs 3 to 5.

4. (a) When it comes to selling, women "seem to outnumber men".

   Write down the expression the writer uses to suggest why the men don't do the selling.

   _____

   _____

   2
   0

   (b) When it comes to buying, there are "as many male customers as female".

   What is the writer's reaction to this? Answer in your own words.

   _____

   2
   0

5. (*a*) The writer gives two examples of "human life" wandering by.
In your own words, explain as fully as you can why the writer:

    (i) disapproves of the "plump medallion man" _____

_____

_____

    (ii) might sympathise with the "succession of polite elderly gentlemen".

_____

_____

(*b*) Explain fully what the writer gains by using the expression "There goes . . ." to introduce these two examples.

_____

_____

Look at Paragraphs 6 and 7.

6. Explain **in your own words** what the writer means by the "serious side" of car boot sales.

_____

_____

7. (*a*) What do each of the following organisations look for at car boot sales?

    (i) Trading Standards _____

    (ii) Police _____

    (iii) Customs and Excise _____

(*b*) Explain what concerns the Environmental Health Officers might have about any food on sale.

_____

_____

8. **Write down** an expression which shows that there are very few concerns about the "serious side" of car boot sales.

_____

2
0

Look at Paragraphs 8 to 14.

9. In Paragraph 8 the writer introduces the idea of giving practical advice.

How does the sentence construction at the beginning of Paragraphs 9 to 14 help to show this?

_____

2
0

10. (*a*) **Write down** the simile or comparison which describes how the antique dealers behave.

_____

2
0

(*b*) Explain what is appropriate about this comparison.

_____

2
1
0

11. From Paragraph 12, **explain in your own words** why:

(*a*) you should "invest in a cheap wallpapering table".

_____

_____

2
1
0

(*b*) you would be "wise to take a friend".

_____

_____

2
1
0

Look at Paragraph 15.

12. ". . . people will buy almost anything . . ."
The writer gives several examples to prove this statement.
Choose any **two** (APART FROM GAMES AND VIDEOS).
In each case explain why the writer thinks it is surprising that anyone should buy them.

(i) _____

_____

2
1
0

(ii) _____

_____

2
1
0

Look at Paragraphs 16 and 17.

13. The writer believes several benefits can be gained from car boot sales. **In your own words** describe two of them.

(i) _____

2
1

(ii) _____

0

14. What do you think the writer is suggesting by her descriptions of the items in Paragraph 17?

_____

2
1
0

15. Why does the writer use ellipsis (. . .) at the end of the final sentence?

_____

2
0

Think about the passage as a whole.

16. Look at the photograph which accompanies the article.
Explain how it shows examples of the following:

(i) the writer's advice being taken _____

_____

(ii) the writer's advice being ignored _____

2
1
0

_____

[Turn over for Question 17 on *Page six*

17. Tick (✓) **one** of the following expressions which you think **best** describes the writer's purpose in this article.

Explain your choice by detailed reference to the text.

to provide information ☐   to entertain ☐

to be thought-provoking ☐

_____

_____

_____

_____

2
1
0

[END OF QUESTION PAPER]

2002 GENERAL

G

0860/403

NATIONAL
QUALIFICATIONS
2002

TUESDAY, 7 MAY
1.00 PM – 1.50 PM

ENGLISH
STANDARD
GRADE
General Level
Reading

Read carefully the passage overleaf. It will help if you read it twice. When you have done so, answer the questions. Use the spaces provided in the Question/Answer booklet.

SCOTTISH
QUALIFICATIONS
AUTHORITY

©

1   The kettle switched itself off the boil with a sharp click. The young man filled the teapot with the steaming water and dropped in a teabag to add to the one already there. He sat the full pot on the formica-topped breakfast bar and made a silly face at his five-year-old daughter who was perched on a stool slowly getting through a bowl of milky porridge. Hearing his wife coming down the stairs from the bathroom he began to refill her mug but instead of entering the bright warm kitchen she lingered in the hall. He could hear her pulling on her heavy coat. She came in saying she had no time, she'd be late for her lift, her heels clattering on the tiled floor. She kissed goodbye to daughter and husband then was off in a whirl of newly-applied perfume and the swish of her clothes and the front door slamming.

2   He sat down on his stool and poured himself another mug of tea. He asked the child how she was doing, was the porridge too hot? She told him gravely that it was OK and went on making a show of blowing on each hot spoonful as she had been shown.

3   He picked up the newspaper that was lying folded open at the Situations Vacant pages. One advert was targeted in a ring of red felt-tip pen. The introduction was in big bold italics: ***"This time last year I was made redundant. Now I own a £150,000 house, drive a BMW and holiday in Bali. If you . . ."*** He opened out the paper and refolded it to the front page to check the headlines. The date he knew already but there it was: exactly one year he had been out of work.

4   Father and daughter chatted brightly as they strolled hand in hand down Allison Street heading for school. She was a talkative child and he would egg her on in her prattle for his own amusement. It was now well into the rush hour: traffic gushed by or fretted at red lights and urgent pedestrians commanded the pavements and crossings. It was bitter cold. He looked down at the girl to reassure himself that she was warmly enough dressed, but there was no need; he was well used to getting her ready. Her round reddened face was the only prey to the cold air and she beamed up at him, quite content.

5   At the last corner before the school's street they both halted in an accustomed way and he squatted down to give her a kiss. She didn't mind the ritual but not outside the gates: her pals might see and that would be too embarrassing. He tugged her knitted hat a little further down her forehead and tucked in a couple of strands of her long reddish hair. They could hear the kids' voices laughing and shouting from the playground. They waved cheerio at the gate and he stood watching until she was inside and with her friends, then he turned away. He was vaguely aware of one or two mothers doing likewise and one or two car doors slamming. With both gloveless hands shoved into the pockets of his cream-coloured raincoat he made for home. Behind him the bell began to sound above and through the high excited voices.

*   *   *   *   *

6   He finished writing the letter and signed his name with a brisk underline, printing it in brackets below, just in case. Picking up the CV from the coffee table he glanced over the familiar details of his education and career. It looked good, he thought, organised, businesslike. His wife had managed to get a couple of dozen of them run off on her word processor at the office. It was the contents that struck him as pointless. What use was it to anyone to know what he had done at school? It was the grown man, someone with work experience, who was on offer, not the schoolboy. Not the kid who'd scuffed along, neither brilliant nor stupid, not the football-daft apprentice smoker who'd put his name to those long-forgotten exam papers then sauntered out carefree into the world. Well, maybe not carefree: he could still

remember some of the burdens and terrors of adolescence that he'd laugh at now. Then there was his five years of selling for the one firm. No problem there; those were good years. Their fruits were holidays abroad, marriage, the house, the baby. Plain sailing until the company had gone bust. Now he was no longer young and upwardly mobile. Not even horizontally mobile: stopped, stuck.

7   Referees. He always wanted to write the name of a football referee but didn't. What did people expect to hear from the names he always supplied—"Don't touch this character, he's a definite no-user"? It was just wee games, this form-filling. He believed it was the interview that would count, if only he could land one.

8   He arranged the letter and CV together, tapping sides and tails until there was no overlap, then folded them in half and in half again. The envelope was ready, briskly typed by his wife on the old manual machine she used for home typing jobs. As he made ready to lick the stamp he stopped suddenly. He'd done it again, folding the sheets in half twice. That was clumsy, unprofessional-looking. The way she'd shown him was much better: folding one third then another so that you only had two folds instead of three. Gingerly, he tried to reopen the envelope but it was stuck fast and the flap ripped jaggedly. He'd have to type another one himself in his laborious two-fingered style. His first go had two mistakes and so he typed another one, slowly, making sure he got everything right.

*   *   *   *   *

9   He kept walking, on past the pillar-box at the corner of their street. That one was definitely unlucky: nothing he had ever posted there had brought good fortune. No, he would carry on to Victoria Road whose offices and air of industry made it feel a more hopeful point of departure. As he reached the main thoroughfare he saw a mail van pull up at the postbox he was heading for and he quickened his pace. He watched the grey-uniformed driver jump down and unlock the red door; he broke into a run. The pillar-box yielded a bulky flow of mail to the driver's hand combing it into his big shapeless bag. The young man handed over his letter with a half-smile although his heart had sunk. One letter in all that flow of paper. And how many were job applications piled randomly, meaninglessly on top of one another? His own would soon be lost in that anonymous crowd. It seemed to him now more than ever like buying a raffle ticket, like doing the football coupon every week. What chance had you got?

10   But it was easy standing here to recall the bustle of business life. It came to him how much he wanted it, that activity. It was more than just something you did to make money: it was the only life he knew and he was missing out on it, standing on the sidelines like a face in the crowd at a football game. If it wasn't for the child, he thought, he wouldn't have the will to keep on trying. He checked his watch: the kids would soon be coming out.

*   *   *   *   *

11   He waited at their corner, hands deep in pockets, his shoulder to the dirty grey sandstone wall. The bell was ringing and he could hear the children streaming out into the playground. When she spotted him she broke into a trot and he retreated round the corner a little to swoop suddenly with a mock roar, bearing her laughing wildly up into his arms. As he set her down he asked quite formally what kind of morning she'd had. She began to speak, and her enthusiasm breathed upwards into his smiling face and beyond in the chill air.

Adapted from the short story "Application" by Michael Munro

[END OF PASSAGE]

[BLANK PAGE]

FOR OFFICIAL USE

G

Total
Mark

0860/404

NATIONAL
QUALIFICATIONS
2002

TUESDAY, 7 MAY
1.00 PM – 1.50 PM

ENGLISH
STANDARD
GRADE
General Level
Reading
Questions

Fill in these boxes and read what is printed below.

Full name of centre

Town

Forename(s)

Surname

Date of birth
Day Month Year

Scottish candidate number

Number of seat

**NB Before leaving the examination room you must give this booklet to the invigilator.
If you do not, you may lose all the marks for this paper.**

SCOTTISH
QUALIFICATIONS
AUTHORITY

©

QUESTIONS

Write your answers in the spaces provided.

Look at Paragraphs 1 to 3.

1. Why did the young man have time to make breakfast for his wife and daughter?

   _____

   Marks **2 ■ 0**

2. From the last sentence in Paragraph 1, **write down two separate words** which suggest his wife was in a hurry.

   [   ]   [   ]

   2 1 0

3. (a) In Paragraph 1, why is "**perched**" a particularly suitable word to describe how the five-year-old girl sat on her stool?

   _____

   _____

   2 1 0

   (b) Give **two** pieces of evidence to show that the daughter treated the business of eating her breakfast seriously.

   (i) _____

   _____

   2 1 0

   (ii) _____

   _____

   2 1 0

4. Why do you think one advert in the newspaper was "targeted in a ring of red felt-tip pen" (Paragraph 3)?

   _____

   _____

   2 1 0

PAGE TOTAL

Marks

Look at Paragraphs 4 and 5.

5. What did the young man enjoy about the walk to school with his daughter? **Answer in your own words.**

_____

_____

2 1 0

6. The writer uses a colon (:) in Paragraph 4 (after "rush hour") and in Paragraph 5 (after "outside the gates").

Tick (✓) the box to show which you think is the correct reason for its use in each case.

2 1 0

	Paragraph 4	*Paragraph 5*
To introduce a quotation		
To elaborate on an idea		
To introduce an explanation		

7. Write down **two** examples of **separate words** the writer has used to convey the idea of "rush hour".

2 1 0

8. "It was bitter cold." (Paragraph 4)

Explain clearly how later in Paragraph 4 the writer makes the cold air seem alive.

_____

_____

2 1 0

[Turn over

PAGE
TOTAL

9. (*a*) Why is the father's kiss described as a "ritual" (Paragraph 5)?

_____

_____ | 2 | 1 | 0 |

(*b*) Which expression earlier in Paragraph 5 helps you to understand the meaning of "ritual"?

_____ | 2 | ■ | 0 |

10. ". . . but not outside the gates . . ." (Paragraph 5)

Using your own words as far as possible, explain why the daughter made this condition.

_____

_____ | 2 | 1 | 0 |

Look at Paragraphs 6 and 7.

11. (*a*) What did the man think "looked good" about his CV?

_____

_____ | 2 | ■ | 0 |

(*b*) What **two** things about "this form-filling" did he think were "pointless"?
In each case explain **why** he thought so.

(i) _____

_____ | 2 | 1 | 0 |

(ii) _____

_____ | 2 | 1 | 0 |

PAGE
TOTAL

Marks

Look at Paragraph 8.

12. (*a*) Why did the man not put the stamp on the envelope?

_____

_____ **2 1 0**

(*b*) "Gingerly, he tried to reopen . . . flap ripped jaggedly."

How does the structure of this sentence emphasise the man's care in reopening the envelope?

_____

_____ **2 1 0**

(*c*) **Write down** the **two** expressions the writer uses in this paragraph to show the contrast between the man's typing skills and his wife's. **2 1 0**

(i) _____

(ii) _____

Look at Paragraphs 9 and 10.

13. Explain clearly why the man chose to post his letter in Victoria Road.

_____

_____

_____ **2 1 0**

14. Explain clearly why "his heart had sunk" (Paragraph 9) when he handed over his letter.

_____

_____ **2 1 0**

[Turn over for Questions 15 to 17 on *Page six*

PAGE
TOTAL

Marks

15. " . . . standing on the sidelines like a face in the crowd at a football game." (Paragraph 10)

Explain how effective you find this simile.

_____

_____   2 1 0

Think about the passage as a whole.

16. Throughout the passage, the man is shown to be thoughtful and caring about his daughter.

What evidence is there of this:

(*a*) in Paragraph 11?   2 1 0

(i) _____

(ii) _____

(*b*) elsewhere in the passage?   2 1 0

(i) _____

(ii) _____

17. Overall, do you feel the story conveys a sense of **hope**, or of **despair**?

Tick (✓) the box to indicate your choice.

Hope	
Despair	

Justify your choice by detailed reference to the text.

_____

_____

_____

_____   2 1 0

[*END OF QUESTION PAPER*]

PAGE TOTAL

G

0860/403

NATIONAL
QUALIFICATIONS
2003

TUESDAY, 6 MAY
1.00 PM – 1.50 PM

ENGLISH
STANDARD GRADE
General Level
Reading
Text

Read carefully the passage overleaf. It will help if you read it twice. When you have done so,
answer the questions. Use the spaces provided in the Question/Answer booklet.

SCOTTISH
QUALIFICATIONS
AUTHORITY

We're out for the Count

Catriona Marchant and her children discover that Dracula has a big stake in Romania's tourist industry.

The door creaked open. A draught of cold air blew up from the stairs to the dark crypt and the hairs on our arms stood on end. The faint light from the flickering candle disappeared, there was a muffled scream, a sound of running footsteps and then some raised voices.

2   My three brave boys looked at each other and Douglas, the middle one, ran from the room. The eldest, Matthew, who had been taunting his younger brothers about being scared five minutes earlier, went a bit white and looked like he was going to change his mind about the visit.

3   We were in Dracula's castle — sited on the remote Tihuta mountain pass where the Victorian Gothic novelist Bram Stoker based the home of his fictitious vampire — two days' carriage ride from Bistrita in northern Transylvania.

4   Downstairs was Count Dracula's coffin in a narrow vault, the walls painted with the dramatic scenes of human victims, wolves, skulls, skeletons and the black-cloaked monster himself, red blood dripping from his pointed fangs. So far on our Romanian holiday the only blood-sucking had been from the mosquitoes in Bucharest. Luckily we had decided to send their father down first as a guinea pig to test out how scary this experience was likely to be for our seven-, five- and two-year-olds.

5   After the screams from the crypt, Matthew decided he would opt for a tour with the light on and I agreed. Even so there was a certain nervousness as we went down the stairs. Suddenly, Matthew let out a blood-curdling scream and jumped a foot in the air. "I've just seen a horrible blue hand with long nails, round the side of that door," he screeched.

6   One vampire hand was quite enough for a seven-year-old. Time for a drink and an ice-cream. As we walked up to the main lobby there was "Vampire" red wine for sale, glass vials of red liquid, wooden stakes and probably some garlic stashed under the counter.

7   As these tacky souvenirs revealed, it wasn't the real Dracula's castle but Hotel Castel Dracula, a three-star hotel built in the mountains to service some nearby ski slopes. The architecture (1980s mock castle) reflected the Dracula movies but the setting amid the dramatic scenery of the Tihuta pass is stunning. The "castle" is circled by bats every night and the surrounding forests have more wild bears and wolves than anywhere else in Europe.

8   Bram Stoker's story has become mixed up with the historical facts as the novelist based his blood-sucking fictional vampire on the 15th century bloodthirsty Prince Vlad Tepes. Vlad was known fondly as Vlad the Impaler.

9   The tourist board makes the most of this confusion between fiction and history, as the worldwide fascination with Dracula lures many a visitor to the country. The most well known sights are the birthplace of Vlad Tepes at the beautiful town of Sighisoara and Bran Castle, commonly known as Dracula's Castle.

10   Bran Castle is certainly dramatic, perched on the edge of a rock peak, its ramparts standing out against the dark mountain backdrop. But as it was the former summer royal residence, parts of it inside seem rather cosy and welcoming. The ruined castle of Rasnov seems a more suitable location for a Dracula film, with 360-degree views of the Carpathian Mountains after a steep walk up the wooded mountain.

11   Matthew did his best to scare the tourists. He had been reading his Dracula books and dressed up in a black cloak, cut out some paper fangs and jumped round corners and down steps.

12   He gained more smiles and laughs than any signs of horror — but then it was a warm, sunny August day. He completed his vampire outfit by choosing wooden daggers for himself and Douglas from the busy craft market to protect us from any blood-sucking monsters that might come our way (apart from mosquitoes).

Cloak and dagger: Alistair and Matthew had a scream fooling around near the birthplace of Vlad Tepes, the "original Dracula"

13   Dracula's Kiss was an extremely alcoholic, bright scarlet drink. This fiery concoction must have contained a large quantity of the local plum brandy, known as palinca. I drank this at the birthplace of Vlad Tepes in Sighisoara. His house is now a restaurant which offers themed menus such as Dracula's tomato soup and fairly average food.

14   Not all the themed food given to the tourists on the hunt for Count Dracula is poor. One of the best and most exciting meals of the holiday was at the Count Dracula Club in Bucharest. Once the children got over the fear of the stuffed bears and stags on the walls and   dog head skulls hanging from the ceiling, the food was fantastic — thick vegetable soup, polenta with stuffed cabbage leaves. The children drank blood orange juice and feasted on thick stew. Down in the cellar was the coffin, with the waiters dressed like vampires and acting for all they were worth.

15   Away from the crypts was hot summer sunshine: we swam in outdoor swimming pools and visited spas with bubbling warm salt lakes. We felt Romania would be a good place to revisit when the boys were older and could hike and camp in the Carpathian wilderness. The most memorable part of our visit to Romania was staying with a delightful family in Sighisoara who loved the children and treated them with kindness as they helped feed their chickens and cook special apple cake.

16   But if we leave the return visit too long things will have changed dramatically. A DraculaLand theme park is planned to be built by a German or American corporation in medieval Sighisoara next year.

17   Local opinion is divided. On the one hand, there is the desire for tourist money and on the other the realisation that the theme park will change the character of the small town forever. If the cobbled streets are lined with fast food chains offering "stakeburgers" and garlic bread — Dracula will be turning in his grave.

Adapted from an article by
Catriona Marchant

[END OF PASSAGE]

[BLANK PAGE]

FOR OFFICIAL USE

G

Total
Mark

0860/404

NATIONAL
QUALIFICATIONS
2003

TUESDAY, 6 MAY
1.00 PM – 1.50 PM

ENGLISH
General Level
Reading
Questions

Fill in these boxes and read what is printed below.

Full name of centre

Town

Forename(s)

Surname

Date of birth
Day Month Year

Scottish candidate number

Number of seat

NB Before leaving the examination room you must give this booklet to the invigilator. If you do not, you may lose all the marks for this paper.

SCOTTISH
QUALIFICATIONS
AUTHORITY

Marks

QUESTIONS

Write your answers in the spaces provided.

Look at Paragraph 1.

1. **In what two ways** does the writer create a frightening atmosphere in the opening sentence?

   (i) _____

   (ii) _____

   2 1 0

2. Explain fully what the writer suggests by using the word "flickering" when describing the candle.

   _____

   _____

   2 1 0

Look at Paragraph 2.

3. "My three brave boys"

   Explain fully why this expression might be considered to be surprising.

   _____

   _____

   2 1 0

4. **Explain in your own words** how Matthew had been treating his brothers.

   _____

   2 ■ 0

Look at Paragraph 3.

5. **Give two pieces of evidence** which suggest that Bram Stoker wrote the novel *Dracula* more than one hundred years ago.

   2 1 0

   (i) _____

   (ii) _____

6. Why does the writer use dashes in Paragraph 3?

   _____

   2 ■ 0

PAGE
TOTAL

Look at Paragraph 4.

7. "Downstairs was Count Dracula's coffin in a narrow vault, the walls painted with the dramatic scenes"

   In what ways does the writer convey the "dramatic scenes" in the vault?

   _____

   _____

   _____   2 1 0

8. What effect does the writer create by using the expression "So far on our Romanian holiday the only blood-sucking had been from the mosquitoes"?

   _____

   _____   2 ■ 0

9. **In your own words** explain fully why their father was sent down first.

   _____

   _____   2 1 0

Look at Paragraphs 5, 6 and 7.

10. **Write down an expression** which shows that Matthew did not complete the tour.

    _____   2 ■ 0

11. **In your own words** what is the writer's attitude to the various goods for sale in the hotel lobby?

    _____

    _____   2 ■ 0

12. **In your own words** what is the writer's opinion of the setting of the Hotel Castel Dracula?

    _____

    _____   2 ■ 0

13. Why does the writer place the word "castle" in inverted commas?

    _____   2 ■ 0

Marks

Look at Paragraphs 8 and 9.

14. What was the real name of the original Dracula?

_____

2 ■ 0

15. Explain **in your own words** how Romania benefits from "this confusion between fiction and history".

_____

_____

2 1 0

Look at Paragraph 10.

16. What contrasting impressions does the writer give of Bran Castle?

_____

_____

2 1 0

Look at Paragraphs 11, 12 and 13.

17. "He gained more smiles and laughs than any signs of horror"

Give two reasons why Matthew was an unconvincing vampire.

_____

_____

2 1 0

18. What does the expression "fiery concoction" suggest about the Dracula's Kiss drink?

_____

_____

2 1 0

PAGE
TOTAL

Marks

Look at Paragraph 14.

19. (*a*) **In your own words explain how** the boys felt at the start of their visit to the Count Dracula Club. **Why** did they feel this way?

_____

_____

| 2 | 1 | 0 |

(*b*) **Write down an expression** which clearly shows that the boys changed their attitude to the visit.

_____

_____

| 2 | ■ | 0 |

Look at Paragraphs 15, 16 and 17.

20. What kind of holiday in Romania might the writer consider in the future?

_____

_____

| 2 | 1 | 0 |

21. (*a*) How does the writer feel about the changes planned for the tourist industry in Romania?

_____

| 2 | ■ | 0 |

(*b*) Explain **in your own words** how the local people feel about the planned changes.

_____

_____

| 2 | 1 | 0 |

(*c*) "Dracula will be turning in his grave."

Why does the writer finish off the final sentence in this way?

_____

_____

| 2 | 1 | 0 |

[Turn over for Question 22 on *Page six*

PAGE TOTAL

Marks

Think about the passage as a whole.

22. "Catriona Marchant and her children discover that Dracula has a big stake in Romania's tourist industry."

Explain fully what is appropriate about this sub-title.

_____

_____

_____ 2 1 0

[*END OF QUESTION PAPER*]

PAGE
TOTAL

G

0860/403

NATIONAL QUALIFICATIONS 2004	WEDNESDAY, 5 MAY 1.00 PM – 1.50 PM	**ENGLISH STANDARD GRADE** General Level Reading Text

Read carefully the passage overleaf. It will help if you read it twice. When you have done so, answer the questions. Use the spaces provided in the Question/Answer booklet.

SCOTTISH QUALIFICATIONS AUTHORITY

Pucker Way to Kiss a Hummingbird

Mark Carwardine puts on lipstick in Arizona for a wild encounter.

SUMMER SPECTACLE:
Thousands of hummingbirds arrive in Arizona every year

1   There's a rather embarrassing tradition in wildlife circles in certain parts of Arizona. Visiting naturalists are encouraged to try to "kiss" a wild hummingbird.

2   This is more of a challenge for men than it is for women – mainly because it involves wearing lots of red lipstick. A dress and high heels are optional, but the redder and thicker the lipstick the better. Hummingbirds drink nectar from flowers that are often bright red and have learned to associate this particular colour with food. They mistake your mouth for one of their favourite plants – at least, that's the theory.

3   Which is how I found myself high in the mountains of South-East Arizona, with puckered lips pointing sky-ward and a crowd of bemused onlookers egging me on.

4   My home for a couple of days was Beatty's Guest Ranch near the Mexico border. Run by Tom and Edith Beatty, the ranch is nearly 6,000ft above sea level, nestling between two enormous peaks, with spectacular views down the valley to the desert below.

5   According to the South-Eastern Arizona Bird Observatory, it is the hottest hummingbird-watching spot in the state. Thousands of "hummers" arrive in April and May and stay until early October. No fewer than 15 different species are found here on a regular basis.

6   Dozens of special hummingbird feeders, looking like upside-down jam jars, are dotted around the ranch. Hanging from trees, bushes, fences and buildings they are full of a simple magic potion (four parts water, one part white sugar) similar to the nectar of hummingbird flowers. Tom and Edith keep the feeders topped up, getting through a mind-boggling 550 2lb bags of sugar in a typical year.

7   There were two feeders outside my bedroom window in the turn-of-the-century self-catering cabin on the forest edge (not a good place to stay if you've seen *Friday The 13th* or *The Blair Witch Project*, but idyllic in every other sense).

8   I will never forget pulling back the curtains on the first morning. There were hummingbirds everywhere, whizzing backwards and forwards past the window like demented bees. Sometimes they paused in front of the sugar-water to feed, either perching or hovering with the immaculate precision of experienced helicopter pilots.

9   Apparently, it's possible to see as many as ten species at the ranch in just half an hour. But even when they stayed still for more than a few moments I had no idea which was which. As they moved around, their colours changed in relation to the angle of the sun. Bird identification is hard enough at the best of times, but this was ridiculous.

10   Take a male hummingbird, for example. When you look at it face-to-face its throat is a fiery scarlet red. But as it turns away the colour shifts – first to orange, then yellow, then blackish-brown and then green. Try identifying that in a hurry, before it turns

into a blur and helicopters away.

11   I think there were Anna's hummingbirds, black-chinned, broad billed, blue-throated, magnificent, red and violet-crowned that morning, but I'm not entirely sure. Later, I asked other bird-watchers about similar-looking hummers around "their" feeding station, but they weren't sure either. I left them bickering over the difference between the sapphire blue throat of a broad-bill and the cobalt blue throat of a blue-throat.

12   The biological advantage of changing colour is that the birds can control the way they look. If a male wants to impress a female he shows his best side, but if he wants to hide from a predator he merely turns away and almost disappears among the greenery.

13   According to Sheri Williamson, hummingbird expert and co-founder of the South-Eastern Arizona Bird Observatory, you can tell them apart by the sound of their wings. Broad-tailed hummingbirds, for example, have a metallic trill to their wingbeats, while male black-chinned hummingbirds make a dull, flat whine.

14   Sheri took me to see a hummingbird in the hand. There's a ringing station, or banding station as they call it in the States, at nearby Sierra Vista. It's open to the public and every weekend the observatory staff rig up a mist-net trap with a tasty-looking sugar-water feeder in the middle. Whenever a hummingbird dares an investigatory hover, a burly member of the observatory team rushes forward, waving his arms around, and ushers the unfortunate bird inside.

15   We caught lots of hummingbirds that day. One was a female black-chinned that squealed when she was caught. It was hard to tell whether this was out of fear or anger ("How could I, so fleet of wing, be caught by this enormous fool?"). We found her abdomen distended with an enormous egg, which Sheri guessed would be laid before nightfall.

16   For a brief moment, I actually held the delicate bundle of feathers in my hand, and

was so nervous about squeezing too hard that she escaped. After hovering above us for a moment, she made a bee-line for the bushes.

17   Hovering hummingbirds draw crowds of naturalists from all over the world to South-East Arizona, but hovering does have one major drawback. Pound for pound, beating your wings 70 times per second uses more energy than any other activity in the animal kingdom. Living life in the fast lane means hummingbirds need a continuous supply of fuel.

18   A typical hummingbird eats around half its own weight in energy-rich nectar every day. To do that it has to keep others away from its favourite foodplants. I spent many hours watching them battle it out at feeding stations. Far from being all sweetness and light, they are little fighter pilots. If they were the size of ravens it wouldn't be safe to walk in the woods.

19   Before I left, there was one thing I had to do. Dutifully, I put on bright red lipstick, took a mouthful of sugar-water, sat back, puckered my lips . . . and waited. Within 30 seconds two hummingbirds came to investigate. Others soon followed.

20   I sat there for an eternity not daring to move. No hummingbird actually drank sugar-water from my mouth (who can blame them?), but several did hover so close I could feel their wingbeats against my cheeks.

21   Strangely, the encounter was every bit as impressive as rubbing shoulders with mountain gorillas in the wilds of Africa or performing slow-motion underwater ballets with dolphins in the Bahamas.

22   Even better, my biggest worry came to nothing – the red lipstick wiped off.

(*Adapted from an article by Mark Carwardine*)

[*END OF PASSAGE*]

[BLANK PAGE]

FOR OFFICIAL USE

G

Total
Mark

0860/404

NATIONAL
QUALIFICATIONS
2004

WEDNESDAY, 5 MAY
1.00 PM – 1.50 PM

ENGLISH
STANDARD GRADE
General Level
Reading
Questions

Fill in these boxes and read what is printed below.

Full name of centre

Town

Forename(s)

Surname

Date of birth
Day Month Year

Scottish candidate number

Number of seat

**NB Before leaving the examination room you must give this booklet to the invigilator.
If you do not, you may lose all the marks for this paper.**

SCOTTISH
QUALIFICATIONS
AUTHORITY

©

QUESTIONS

Write your answers in the spaces provided.

Look at Paragraphs 1 and 2.

1. **Write down a word** from Paragraph 1 that suggests naturalists might be reluctant to kiss a hummingbird.

   _____

   2 ■ 0

2. Why are the hummingbirds attracted to someone wearing bright red lipstick?

   _____

   _____

   2 1 0

3. Why do you think the writer uses the word "theory" in Paragraph 2?

   _____

   2 ■ 0

Look at Paragraphs 3 and 4.

4. Where **exactly** did the writer first meet the hummingbirds?

   _____

   _____

   2 1 0

Look at Paragraphs 5 and 6.

5. Thousands of "hummers" (Paragraph 5)

   Why has the writer put the word "hummers" in inverted commas?

   _____

   _____

   2 ■ 0

Marks

PAGE
TOTAL

Marks

6. "Hanging from trees, bushes, fences and buildings they are full of a simple magic potion . . . flowers." (Paragraph 6)

   Identify and comment on the effect of **two features** of the structure of this sentence.

   (i) _____

   _____   2   1   0

   (ii) _____

   _____   2   1   0

7. **Write down an expression** from Paragraph 6 which tells you that the writer is surprised by the amount of sugar used.

   _____   2   ■   0

Look at Paragraphs 7 and 8.

8. What do the expressions "whizzing" and "like demented bees" tell you about the movement of the hummingbirds?

   _____

   _____   2   1   0

9. **Write down an expression** which shows that the writer admires the flying skills of the hummingbird.

   _____   2   ■   0

Look at Paragraphs 9 and 10.

10. **In your own words** write down **two** reasons why the writer found bird identification "ridiculous".   2   1   0

    (i) _____

    (ii) _____

PAGE TOTAL

Marks

Look at Paragraphs 11 and 12.

11. What does the writer's use of the word "bickering" tell you about his attitude to the bird watchers?

_____

2 ■ 0

12. **In your own words** give **two** reasons why hummingbirds change their colour.

(i) _____

(ii) _____

2 1 0

Look at Paragraphs 13 to 15.

13. How does Sheri Williamson tell the difference between hummingbirds?

_____

_____

2 1 0

14. Comment on the writer's use of the expression "hummingbird in the hand".

_____

_____

2 1 0

15. "Whenever a hummingbird dares an investigatory hover, a burly member of the observatory team rushes forward, waving his arms around" (Paragraph 14)

How does this description create effective contrasts?

(i) _____

2 ■ 0

(ii) _____

2 ■ 0

Look at Paragraph 16.

16. What does the expression "I actually held" tell you about how the writer felt when he held the hummingbird?

_____

_____

2 ■ 0

PAGE
TOTAL

Marks

Look at Paragraphs 17 and 18.

17. "Living life in the fast lane means hummingbirds need a continuous supply of fuel." (Paragraph 17)

    Explain the effectiveness of this image.

    _____

    _____

    _____   2 1 0

18. **In your own words**, what **two** new impressions does the writer give of the hummingbird in Paragraph 18?

    _____

    _____   2 1 0

Look at Paragraphs 19 to 22.

19. "Dutifully, I put on bright red lipstick . . . puckered my lips . . . and waited." (Paragraph 19)

    Identify and comment on any **one feature** of structure **or** punctuation in this sentence.

    _____

    _____

    _____   2 1 0

20. **Write down an expression** from Paragraph 20 which tells us the writer felt he waited for a long time.

    _____   2 ■ 0

21. **In your own words** what does the writer's use of the word "Strangely" tell you about his reaction to the encounter with the hummingbirds?

    _____   2 ■ 0

[Turn over for Questions 22 and 23 on *Page six*

PAGE
TOTAL

Marks

Think about the passage as a whole.

22. From the passage **write down an example** of the writer's use of humour.

Explain why it is effective.

_____

_____

_____ 2 1 0

23. Overall how do you think the writer feels about his experience with the humming-birds?

Support your answer by referring to the passage.

_____

_____

_____ 2 1 0

[END OF QUESTION PAPER]

PAGE
TOTAL

2000 CREDIT

C

0860/405

NATIONAL QUALIFICATIONS 2000	TUESDAY, 16 MAY 2.30 PM – 3.20 PM	ENGLISH STANDARD GRADE Credit Level Reading Text

Read carefully the passage overleaf. It will help if you read it twice. When you have done so, answer the questions. Use the spaces provided in the Question/Answer booklet.

A writer reflects on the changes which have taken place in a coastal area of southern Ireland.

1   You can walk along the strand all the way from Ardmore to the derelict one-storey Georgian house on the cliff. You pass Ballyquin on the way, a little cove that has a car park now. The sand is smooth and damp, here and there marbled with grey, or dusty dry, depending on whether you choose to walk by the sea or closer to the cliffs. There are shrimps and anemones in the rock pools, and green slithery seaweed as you pass the rocky places by. The cliffs are clay, easy game for the encroaching winter waves. Washed timber and plastic bottles are the flotsam of the shingle.

2   A woman pushes a bicycle, the buckets that hang from its handlebars heavy with seafood from the rocks. A horse and cart carries gravel or seaweed back to Ballyquin. In the nineteen thirties this strand was always empty, except on the rare days when a solitary figure could be seen, suddenly there out of nowhere, clambering down the cliff-face. Clothes were weighed down with a stone and then he ran naked to the sea.

3   Inland a little way, not always visible from the strand, is Ballyquin House, four-square and architecturally simple, cream-washed when the O'Reillys lived there. Mrs O'Reilly, a widow, attired always in black, was a woman whose unobtrusive presence called for, but did not demand, respect. All the old decencies were in the woman that Mrs O'Reilly was: you hardly had to look at her to know she would rather not live at all than live dubiously, in some mean-spirited way. Her two children, Biddy and Henry, were in their early twenties. Her brother, a silent man who kept his hat on, worked the farm. An old uncle—known as Blood-an'-Ouns because he so often used the expression—got drunk in Ardmore every Easter but otherwise did not touch a drop.

4   Henry O'Reilly was known locally as the laziest man in Ireland, but in my childhood opinion he was also the nicest. Red-haired and already becoming bulky, he took me with him on the cart to the creamery and on the way back we would stop at a crossroads half-and-half—a shop that was a grocery as well as a public house. He had a bottle of stout himself, and bought me a lemonade and biscuits. He would settle his elbows on the counter, exchanging whatever news there was with the woman who served us. "Give the boy another mineral," he'd say, and he'd order another packet of biscuits for me, or a Cadbury's bar. Eventually the horse would take us slowly on, lingering through the sunshine, Henry O'Reilly having a nap, the reins in my charge. Most of the day it took, to go to the creamery and back.

5   Henry O'Reilly made me an aeroplane, nailing together a few scraps of wood, which he then painted white. He showed me how to snare a rabbit and how to shoot one. When I was eight or so I weeded a field of turnips with him, a task that didn't require much energy because we stopped whenever a new story began, and Henry O'Reilly went in for stories. At twelve o'clock we returned to the farmhouse and sat down in the kitchen to a meal of potatoes, which were tumbled out on to a newspaper in the centre of the table.

6   The O'Reillys' land stretched right to the cliff edge, but the O'Reillys rarely ventured on to the strand, as country people who live by the sea so often don't. There were cows to milk, and feed to be boiled for the hens, and crops to be harvested, the churns of milk delivered. The front door of the house was never opened, the rooms on either side of it and the bedrooms above only entered when dusting took place.

7   There is a glen where the strand ends, separating the land that was once the O'Reillys' from woods that have become dense. And there, much closer to the cliff edge than the O'Reillys', is the derelict house. The woods stretch for miles behind it and somewhere in the middle of them lived a man with rheumy eyes called Paddy Lyndon. In a tumbled-down outbuilding there was an old motor-car with brass headlamps—one of the first, Paddy Lyndon averred, that had taken to the roads in Ireland. "Are you sober, Paddy?" Henry O'Reilly would always greet Paddy Lyndon when they met, an enquiry that received no response.

8   Glencairn House the derelict place was called when first I knew it fifty years ago. It was owned then by an Englishman who'd left Ireland during the Troubles and only rarely returned—a Mr Fuge who'd built a dream house, not knowing that dreams are not to be trusted. "As good a man as ever stood on two feet," Paddy Lyndon said. "A man that never owed a debt." Through the cracks of the efficiently boarded windows nothing could be distinguished in the darkness that kept the rooms' secrets. A briar rose trailed through a patch of garden, gone as wild as the surrounding gorse. I liked the mystery of this good Englishman who'd left his property in Paddy Lyndon's charge, who only stayed for twenty minutes when he came back. "There's stories about Fuge I could tell you," Henry O'Reilly said, but he never did because he never got round to making them up.

9   But it is the sea, not houses or people, that dominates the strand. To the sea, and the sand and rocks that receive it, belong the images you carry with you when you pass on to the woody slopes of the glen, and the barley fields. The waves call the tune of the place, in a murmur or a passionate crescendo. There's salt on the inland air, and seagulls strut the furrows.

10   Jellyfish float in when they're in a mood for it. Once in a while there's a trawler on the horizon. The sea on the turn's the best, the sand left perfect or waiting to be doused. It's easier to skim pebbles over the water when it's unruffled—as it was the time I nearly drowned, causing panic one hot afternoon.

11   Two generations on, the shells are as they've always been; so are the paw-prints of a dog. The dog has a branch of brown seaweed trailing from its jaws, and takes no notice when he's called. People nod as they pass, or say hullo. Children build castles and watch them being washed away, old men paddle. A primus stove splutters. It's out of the question that a naked figure will run into the sea.

12   Still no one lives in the derelict house. The boards that once so curtly covered the windows, a kind of packing case around the house, have fallen away. You can see the rooms now, but if ever there was furniture all of it has gone. The wall beside the avenue has collapsed.

[Turn over

13   The O'Reillys' farmhouse is different too. Years ago Biddy made her way to Chicago, Henry married into Ardmore. Mrs O'Reilly and her brother, the old uncle too, are long since dead. The house is no longer in the family, the land is differently farmed.

14   There is no nostalgia here, only remembered facts—and the point that passing time has made: the strand is still the strand, taking change and another set of customs in its stride, as people and houses cannot. While you walk its length, there is something comforting in that.

Adapted from *Excursions in the Real World* by William Trevor

[END OF PASSAGE]

FOR OFFICIAL USE

C

Total Mark

0860/406

| NATIONAL QUALIFICATIONS 2000 | TUESDAY, 16 MAY 2.30 PM – 3.20 PM | ENGLISH STANDARD GRADE Credit Level Reading Questions |

Fill in these boxes and read what is printed below.

Full name of centre

Town

Forename(s)

Surname

Date of birth
Day Month Year

Scottish candidate number

Number of seat

NB Before leaving the examination room you must give this booklet to the invigilator. If you do not, you may lose all the marks for this paper.

SCOTTISH QUALIFICATIONS AUTHORITY

MCB 0860/406 6/3/43020

QUESTIONS

Write your answers in the spaces provided.

Look at Paragraphs 1 and 2.

1. In what way is the sand different at either edge of the strand?

    _____

    _____

2. Explain fully why the cliffs are described as "easy game" for the waves in winter.

    _____

    _____

3. (*a*) **In your own words**, explain the difference between the strand today and the strand in the nineteen thirties.

    _____

    _____

    (*b*) What has been provided in the area which might have contributed to this difference?

    _____

Page two

Look at Paragraphs 3 to 5.

4. **Quote** an expression which indicates that Mrs O'Reilly was not a very noticeable woman.

_____

_____

2
0

5. What was one of the "old decencies" which the writer felt was obvious in Mrs O'Reilly?

   Answer in your own words.

_____

_____

2
1
0

6. The writer uses the dash (—) in the last sentence of Paragraph 3 and the second sentence of Paragraph 4.

   Explain their different function in each case.

   (i) **Paragraph 3** _____

   _____

2
0

   (ii) **Paragraph 4** _____

   _____

2
0

7. Give **three** pieces of evidence which suggest why Henry O'Reilly would be:

   (a) **known locally** as the laziest man in Ireland.

   (i) _____

   (ii) _____

   (iii) _____

2
1
0

   (b) **thought by the writer** to be the nicest man in Ireland.

   (i) _____

   (ii) _____

   (iii) _____

2
1
0

[Turn over

Look at Paragraphs 6 to 8.

8. **In your own words**, explain **fully** why the O'Reillys, like other country people, "rarely ventured on to the strand".

_____

_____

_____

2
1
0

9. "Glencairn House the derelict place was called . . ."
   Give **two** examples from Paragraphs 7 and 8 which support this description.

   (i) _____

   (ii) _____

2
1
0

10. Explain **in your own words** why the writer describes Mr Fuge as "not knowing that dreams are not to be trusted".

_____

_____

_____

2
1
0

11. Why did Paddy Lyndon think Mr Fuge was a good man?

_____

2
0

12. Why might it seem strange that Mr Fuge had "left his property in Paddy Lyndon's charge"?

_____

_____

_____

2
1
0

Look at Paragraphs 9 to 11.

13. "But it is the sea, not houses or people, that dominates the strand."

    (*a*) Explain how this sentence is an effective link between the earlier part of the passage (Paragraphs 3 to 8) and the rest of Paragraphs 9 to 11.

      _____

      _____

      _____

2
1
0

    (*b*) Explain how the **structure** of the second sentence of Paragraph 9 ("To the sea . . . barley fields.") emphasises the importance of the sea.

      _____

      _____

2
1
0

    (*c*) Quote **two examples** of the writer's **word-choice** in the rest of Paragraph 9 which continue to emphasise the dominance of the sea.

      (i) _____

      (ii) _____

2
1
0

14. What **two** contrasting impressions of the sea does the writer convey in Paragraph 10?

    _____

    _____

2
1
0

15. Why do you think the writer **repeats** the reference to "a naked figure" at this point?

    _____

    _____

2
1
0

[Turn over for Questions 16 and 17 on *Page six*

Look at Paragraphs 12 to 14.

16. (a) What evidence does the writer give in Paragraphs 12 and 13 to illustrate the changes in **both** people and houses?

_____

_____

_____

2
1
0

(b) **In your own words**, describe the feelings he expresses about the strand in the last paragraph.

_____

_____

2
1
0

Think about the passage as a whole.

17. The writer's purpose in this article is to **describe** and **reflect upon** the strand, its surroundings and people.

Several features of his writing help him to achieve his purpose—for example word-choice, selective detail, figures of speech, structure etc.

Select **two** features and, by referring to an example of each, show how they help to make his writing effective.

(i) _____

_____

_____

2
1
0

(ii) _____

_____

_____

2
1
0

[END OF QUESTION PAPER]

2001 CREDIT

C

0860/405

| NATIONAL QUALIFICATIONS 2001 | MONDAY, 14 MAY 2.30 PM – 3.20 PM | ENGLISH STANDARD GRADE Credit Level Reading Text |

Read carefully the passage overleaf. It will help if you read it twice. When you have done so, answer the questions. Use the spaces provided in the Question/Answer booklet.

In this extract the narrator reflects on the first visit of an aunt and cousin.

1   They didn't come to England till 1962. It was the "*n*"-th year of preparations for a visit that always, in the end, failed to happen.

2   I'd just arrived home for autumn half-term and at first I didn't believe what I was told—that their plane had touched down at the airport—and I wasn't convinced till I saw for myself the black Humber Hawk taxi come swinging up the drive, axles creaking, carrying its two passengers in the back, one swathed in furs.

3   "It's your cousin," my mother told me unnecessarily, nervous beside me on the top step as we made a little reception committee with my father for our guests none of us had ever seen.

4   The driver opened the back door of the taxi and my "aunt", as we referred to her— really my mother's aunt's daughter—divested herself of the travelling rugs. She hazarded a foot out on to the gravel—in a pointy crocodile shoe—as if she were testing the atmosphere. She emerged dressed in a waisted black cashmere overcoat with a fur collar and strange scalloped black kid-skin gloves like hawking gauntlets.

5   I saw my mother noting again the black stiletto-heeled shoes with their red piping. The face we'd never seen was hidden under a broad-brimmed black felt hat, which I felt none of the women *we* knew in our closed circle would have had the courage to put on their heads.

6   "Hi!" my aunt greeted us in a surprisingly light, sprightly voice, unpinning the furs across her shoulders.

7   A shadow moved behind her in the car. Behind them both the driver was lifting half a dozen assorted white suitcases out of the boot. My mother drew in her breath.

8   "It's so cold!" my aunt called to us from under her hat. "Brr, I can't take it like this!"

9   Then she smiled—at the three of us, each in turn—quite charmingly.

10   My mother relaxed, realising our guest was only being eccentric, not insulting.

11   "Well I hope you'll be warm *here*," my mother told her by way of introduction, with just a little "tone" in her voice.

12   I could see better now. Beneath her discreetly black coat my aunt had very long, slender, shapely legs. Behind her, her son—my cousin Walter—ventured unsurely into the hall.

13   "Unfortunately," my mother addressed the face under the hat, "you've come at the very coldest season."

14   "Oh, I know I'll be very warm here, I can tell already," my aunt assured her with another toothpaste advertisement smile, throwing her furs on to a chair like a film star. "Very comfortable. I've so wanted to see you all, you can't imagine."

15   My mother smiled—cautiously—and my father closed the door.

16   "Do come and have some tea, both of you," he said.

17   He was forever at a loss with guests to Oakdene, my father: now for some reason a smile was starting to break on his reserved banker's "business" face my mother and I were so used to living with.

18   I examined my cousin surreptitiously while I helped my father carry the cases to the foot of the staircase—while *he* just stood there, doing nothing. He was odd-looking, I saw. He had a triangular-shaped face with a bony chin, and he was bloodlessly, alarmingly pale. He stood with his shoulders hunched; very arched eyebrows and flat ears set close against his head added to the pixie-ness of his appearance. What made me think him odder still was his not seeming to match at all with his elegant (and, from what I could see, pretty) mother. (How ugly must his father be, I wondered, to correct the balance of heredity?) He was several inches shorter than I was, although I knew we were the same age (eleven, if the year was 1962). His height—or his lack of height—was another disappointment, and also his thinness. I'd expected he would look stolid, and assertive, and the very picture of glowing health. Instead the eyes in his pale face flitted among us, like a prying spinster's, missing nothing.

19   "Did you have a nice flight?" my mother asked, with controlled politeness. "I can't remember where . . ."

20   "Oh, we've been everywhere! Everywhere!" my aunt explained, pausing at the hatstand to remove her wide-brimmed hat. She seemed to take off twenty years with it and suddenly I felt they were a generation apart, she and my mother. My aunt pulled at her hair—becomingly blonde (dyed, I think it must have been) and smartly cut—with the tips of her fingers. In her black crocodile shoes and with her black lizard bag and the long kid gloves tucked into the pockets of her coat, she looked very expensive. I was utterly fascinated.

21   "Paris. Como. Rome." She crossed them off on those creamed, manicured fingers with their scarlet nails. (She was making little perfume trails whenever she moved.) "Where else, now? Antibes, of course. And we saw a little bit of Switzerland. That *was* cold!"

22   She walked ahead of us into the sitting-room and made for the fireplace and the crackling log fire.

23   "Capri. That was just heaven. And Naples, of course."

24   My mother watched her from the hall. "Of course," she repeated, just to herself, under her breath.

25   Their visit to us was bad timing. We were having a very cold snap, and in another week—when our guests would have gone—it would be November, then December after that, with Christmas fir trees for sale in the village shops. We were to be their last stop before they flew home. I suppose we were a family obligation. Or—were we really something else, a different kind of invitation to their travellers' curiosity . . . ?

26   In our sitting-room my aunt seemed very exotic, and rather theatrical: not at all like my staid "county" mother with her scrubbed grouse-moor complexion. For "housewives", how unalike they seemed! On a scale of prettiness my aunt might have scored seven marks out of ten: she certainly "made the most of what she had"—as my mother would say of certain women she didn't quite approve of, because (another of her expressions) they "tried too hard".

[Turn over

27   When my aunt took off her coat she was wearing a canary silk suit underneath, and my mother looked most uncomfortable in the other big wing-chair, pulling her tweed skirt over her knees and tugging at the pearls round her throat. My cousin Walter sat, not where he was invited to, but on a hard-bottomed shield-back chair from where he could observe all our different posturings with his range of vision clear and unimpeded.

28   My aunt burst the seal on a pack of cigarettes and leaned forward in her chair to catch the flame from my father's lighter. I saw my mother taking a suddenly critical view of the situation. Her face was set in a way I wasn't unfamiliar with.

29   "You'll have some tea, Stella?"

30   My aunt nodded through the thick blue fog of cigarette smoke. I noticed how speedily her eyes were racing round our sitting-room, as Walter's had done earlier, recording our possessions.

31   Like my mother I was already starting to feel not at all at my ease: almost—silly to say—like a stranger here in my own home.

Adapted from a short story by Ronald Frame

[END OF PASSAGE]

FOR OFFICIAL USE

C

Total Mark

0860/406

NATIONAL
QUALIFICATIONS
2001

MONDAY, 14 MAY
2.30 PM – 3.20 PM

ENGLISH
STANDARD GRADE
Credit Level
Reading
Questions

Fill in these boxes and read what is printed below.

Full name of centre

Town

Forename(s)

Surname

Date of birth
Day Month Year

Scottish candidate number

Number of seat

**NB Before leaving the examination room you must give this booklet to the invigilator.
If you do not, you may lose all the marks for this paper.**

SCOTTISH
QUALIFICATIONS
AUTHORITY

MCB 0860/406 6/43320

QUESTIONS

Write your answers in the spaces provided.

Look at Paragraphs 1 to 3.

1. **In your own words**, explain fully why the narrator at first didn't believe that "their plane had touched down at the airport".

_____

_____

2
1
0

2. What finally convinced him it was true?

_____

_____

2
1
0

3. (*a*) Why was the narrator's mother "nervous"?

_____

_____

2
1
0

   (*b*) What evidence is there of her nervousness?

_____

2
0

Look at Paragraphs 4 and 5.

4. (*a*) What impression of the aunt do you get from the writer's choice of the words "divested", "hazarded" and "emerged" to describe her movements?

_____

2
0

   (*b*) What is added to this impression by his description of what she was wearing?

_____

2
0

5. What is the function of the dashes (—) used in Paragraph 4?

_____

2
0

Look at Paragraphs 6 to 15.

6. "My mother drew in her breath." (Paragraph 7)

   (*a*) What does this tell you about her feelings?

   _____

   (*b*) What caused her to react this way?

   _____

   _____

7. Explain **in your own words** why the mother, in welcoming the aunt, spoke with just a little "tone" in her voice.

   _____

   _____

8. (*a*) What impression of cousin Walter is given in Paragraph 12?

   _____

   (*b*) How does the writer prepare us for this image of Walter earlier in this section?

   _____

   _____

Look at Paragraphs 16 to 18.

9. Explain **in your own words**:

   (*a*) in what **two** ways the father reacted to the guests;

   _____

   _____

   (*b*) why in each case this was unusual.

   _____

   _____

[Turn over

10. **Quote** an expression which shows that the narrator tried to find out about his cousin in a secretive way.

_____

2
0

11. "He was odd-looking . . ."

Explain **in your own words** what the narrator seemed to think was the strangest thing about his cousin.

_____

_____

2
1
0

12. What does the last sentence of Paragraph 18 tell us about Walter's character?

_____

2
0

Look at Paragraphs 19 to 24.

13. **Using your own words**, explain why the narrator gave so many details about his aunt.

_____

_____

2
1
0

14. " 'Of course,' she repeated, just to herself, under her breath."

What does this suggest the mother thought of the aunt's tales of travel?

_____

2
0

Look at Paragraph 25.

15. **According to the narrator**, what were the **two** possible reasons for the relatives' visits? **Answer in your own words**.

(i) _____

_____

2
1
0

(ii) _____

_____

2
1
0

Look at Paragraphs 26 to 31.

16. ". . . how unalike they seemed!"

    Give details of **two** obvious contrasts between the aunt and the mother.

    (i) _____

    _____

    (ii) _____

    _____

17. What does the writer's use of the word "posturings" (Paragraph 27) tell you about the behaviour of the people in the room?

    _____

    _____

Think about the passage as a whole.

18. Why do you think the writer makes frequent use of brackets throughout the passage?

    _____

    _____

19. The narrator began to feel "like a stranger" in his own home. (Paragraph 31)

    By close reference to the text, show how his feelings towards his aunt changed.

    _____

    _____

    _____

[END OF QUESTION PAPER]

[BLANK PAGE]

2002 CREDIT

C

0860/405

<table>
<tr><td>NATIONAL QUALIFICATIONS 2002</td><td>TUESDAY, 7 MAY 2.30 PM – 3.20 PM</td><td>ENGLISH STANDARD GRADE Credit Level Reading Text</td></tr>
</table>

Read carefully the passage overleaf. It will help if you read it twice. When you have done so, answer the questions. Use the spaces provided in the Question/Answer booklet.

SCOTTISH
QUALIFICATIONS
AUTHORITY

©

This passage concerns a store detective's encounter with an unusual shoplifter.

1   Sometimes on dark winter mornings he watched them before the doors were opened: pressing their hands and faces against the glass, a plague of moths wanting in to the light. But you couldn't look at them like that, as an invading swarm. To do the job – which was under threat anyway because of security guards and surveillance cameras – you had to get in among them, make yourself invisible. You had to blend in, pretend to be one of them, but you also had to observe them, you had to see the hand slipping the "Game Boy" into the sleeve. Kids wore such loose clothes nowadays, baggy jeans and jogging tops two sizes too big for them. It was the fashion, but it meant they could hide their plunder easily. You had to watch the well-dressed gentlemen as well – the Crombie coat and the briefcase could conceal a fortune in luxury items. When it came down to it, you were a spy.

2   He was in the food hall and they were rushing around him. He picked up a wire basket and strolled through the vegetables, doing his best to look interested in a packet of Continental Salad, washed and ready to use. It was easy to stop taking anything in and let the shopping and the shoplifting happen around you, a blur, an organism, an animal called The Public. The Public was all over the shop: poking its nose into everything; trying on the clean new underwear; squirting the testers on its chin, on its wrists, behind its ears; wriggling its fingers into the gloves; squeezing its warm, damp feet into stiff, new shoes; tinkering with the computers; thumbing the avocados.

3   He was watching a grey-haired lady dressed in a sagging blue raincoat, probably in her sixties, doing exactly that. The clear blue eyes, magnified by thick lenses, looked permanently shocked. A disappointed mouth, darkened by a plum-coloured lipstick, floundered in a tight net of wrinkles. There was something in her movements that was very tense, yet she moved slowly, as if she had been stunned by some very bad news.

4   She put down the avocados – three of them, packaged in polythene – as if she'd just realised what they were and didn't need them. He followed her as she made her way to the express pay-point and took her place in the queue. He stacked his empty basket and waited on the other side of the cash-points, impersonating a bewildered husband waiting for the wife he'd lost sight of. He watched her counting her coins from a small black purse. The transaction seemed to fluster her, as if she might not have enough money to pay for the few things she'd bought. A tin of lentil soup. An individual chicken pie. One solitary tomato. Maybe she did need the avocados – or something else.

5   Some shoplifters used the pay-point: it was like declaring something when you went through customs, in the hope that the real contraband would go unnoticed. An amateur tactic. It was easy to catch someone with a conscience, someone who wanted to be caught.

6   He ambled behind her to the escalator down to Kitchen and Garden. When she came off the escalator, she waited at the bottom, as if not sure where to find what she was looking for. He moved away from her to the saucepans and busied himself opening up a three-tiered vegetable steamer, then he put the lid back on hastily to follow her to the gardening equipment. She moved past the lawn-mowers and the sprinklers until she came to a display of seed packets.

7   It wasn't often you had this kind of intuition about somebody, but as soon as he saw her looking at the seeds, he was certain she was going to steal them. He moved closer to her, picked up a watering can and weighed it in his hand, as if this was somehow a way of testing it, then he saw her dropping packet after packet into the bag. He followed her to the door and outside, then he put his hand on her shoulder. When she turned round he showed her his identity card. Already she was shaking visibly. Her red-veined cheeks had taken on a hectic colour and tears loomed behind her outraged blue eyes . . .

8   "Please," she said, "arrest me. Before I do something worse."

9   He took her back inside and they made the long journey to the top of the store in silence. For the last leg of it he took her through Fabrics – wondering if they might be taken for a couple, a sad old couple shopping together in silence – and up the back staircase so that he wouldn't have to march her through Admin.

10   It was depressing to unlock the door of his cubby-hole, switch the light on and see the table barely big enough to hold his kettle and his tea things, the one upright chair, the barred window looking out on a fire-escape and the wall-mounted telephone. He asked her to take the packets of seeds out of her bag and put them on the table. She did so, and the sight of the packets, with their gaudy coloured photographs of flowers, made her clench her hand into a fist.

11   He told her to take a seat while he called security, but when he turned away from her she let out a thin wail that made him recoil from the phone. She had both her temples between her hands, as if afraid her head might explode. She let out another shrill wail. It ripped out of her like something wild kept prisoner for years. It seemed to make the room shrink around them.

12   She wailed again – a raw outpouring of anger and loss.

13   "Look, you don't seem like a habitual shoplifter . . ."

14   She blurted out that she'd never stolen anything in her life before, but it was hard to make out the words because she was sobbing, and coughing at the same time, her meagre body shuddering as if an invisible man had taken her by the shoulders and was shaking her violently.

15   "I'm sure it was just absent-mindedness. You intended to pay for these." He motioned with a hand to the scattered packets of seeds on the table, but she was having none of it.

16   "No, I stole them. I don't even like gardening." The words came out in spurts between her coughs and sobs but there was no stopping her now that she'd started: "It's overgrown, weeds everywhere. It was him who did it. He was mad about his garden. He spent all his time, morning till night, out in all weathers."

17   Relieved that she was talking rather than wailing, he let her talk. Her husband had been obsessed with his garden. It had been his way of getting away – from her, from everyone and everything. He'd withdrawn from the world into his flowering shrubs and geraniums. She hardly saw him, and when he'd died all there was left of him was his garden. Now the weeds were taking over. When she'd seen the seed packets, with their pictures of dahlias and pansies and rhododendrons . . . It made a kind of sense. Why had she stolen them rather than pay for them? He should have known better than to ask. He got the whole story of her financial hardship now that she was on her own, including the cost of the funeral. It was an expensive business, dying.

[Turn over

18   When she'd finished, she fished a small white handkerchief from her coat pocket to wipe the tears from her eyes. It was the way she did this that reminded him of his mother, the way she had to move her glasses out of the way to get the handkerchief to her eyes.

19   "What are you going to do with me?" she said.

Adapted from the short story "An Invisible Man" by Brian McCabe

[*END OF PASSAGE*]

FOR OFFICIAL USE

C

Total
Mark

0860/406

NATIONAL
QUALIFICATIONS
2002

TUESDAY, 7 MAY
2.30 PM – 3.20 PM

ENGLISH
STANDARD GRADE
Credit Level
Reading
Questions

Fill in these boxes and read what is printed below.

Full name of centre

Town

Forename(s)

Surname

Date of birth
Day Month Year

Scottish candidate number

Number of seat

**NB Before leaving the examination room you must give this booklet to the invigilator.
If you do not, you may lose all the marks for this paper.**

SCOTTISH
QUALIFICATIONS
AUTHORITY

MCB 0860/406 6/43270

QUESTIONS

Write your answers in the spaces provided.

Look at Paragraph 1.

1. What **two** things were required of the store detective in order to do his job well?

   (i) _____

   (ii) _____

2. (a) Explain what concerns the detective had about:

   (i) kids;

   _____

   _____

   (ii) well-dressed gentlemen.

   _____

   _____

   (b) Why do you think **the writer** uses "kids" and "well-dressed gentlemen" as examples?

   _____

   _____

3. Explain why it is appropriate to describe the shoppers as "a plague".

   _____

   _____

Look at Paragraphs 2 to 4.

4. What did the detective do to avoid being noticed in the food hall?

   _____

   _____

Marks

2 1

2 1

2 1

2 1

2 1

2 1

Marks

5. Look closely at the final sentence of Paragraph 2.

Identify any **one technique** used by the writer and explain how it helps to create the impression that "The Public was all over the shop".

_____

_____

_____   2 1 0

6. (*a*) What was the woman doing when the detective first noticed her?

_____   2 ■ 0

(*b*) **Quote** the expression which best suggests why he followed her to the pay-point.

_____

_____   2 ■ 0

7. **In your own words** describe what the detective did to avoid being noticed at the pay-point.

_____

_____   2 1 0

8. In Paragraph 4, how does the writer emphasise that the woman had bought "few things"

(i) by word-choice?

_____

_____   2 1 0

(ii) by sentence structure?

_____

_____   2 1 0

[Turn over

PAGE
TOTAL

Look at Paragraphs 5 to 8.

9. (*a*) The writer compares some shoplifters' use of the pay-point to "declaring something when you went through customs".

Explain fully why this is an appropriate comparison.

_____

_____

_____

2 1

(*b*) Quote an expression which shows that the store detective thought shoplifters were usually unsuccessful when they used the pay-point.

_____

_____

2 ■ 0

10. "It wasn't often you had this kind of intuition . . ."

How does the rest of Paragraph 7 help to explain the meaning of "intuition"?

_____

_____

2 1 0

11. " 'Please,' she said, 'arrest me. Before I do something worse.' "

Tick (✓) the appropriate box to show which of the following **best** describes your reaction to this statement.

surprised	
intrigued	
not surprised	
sympathetic	

Justify your choice by **close reference to the text**.

_____

_____

_____

_____

2 1 0

Look at Paragraphs 9 and 10.

12. **In your own words** give **two** pieces of evidence which suggest the detective felt some sympathy towards the woman.

    (i) _____

    _____

    2 1 0

    (ii) _____

    _____

    2 1 0

13. The detective found the sight of his cubby-hole "depressing".
    Explain how the writer continues this idea in Paragraph 10.

    _____

    _____

    2 1 0

Look at Paragraphs 11 to 13.

14. Quote a comparison from this section which shows how emotional or upset the woman was, and explain how effective you find it.

    _____

    _____

    _____

    2 1 0

Look at Paragraphs 14 to 16.

15. What further evidence is there in this section that the detective showed some sympathy towards the woman?

    _____

    _____

    2 ■ 0

[Turn over for Questions 16 to 19 on *Page six*

PAGE
TOTAL

Marks

Look at Paragraphs 17 and 18.

16. Explain clearly why the woman's need for the seed packets "made a kind of sense".

_____

_____

_____ 2 1 0

Think about the passage as a whole.

17. In Paragraph 12 the writer describes the woman's wailing as a "raw outpouring of **anger** and **loss**".

Explain clearly how these emotions relate to her relationship with her husband.

_____

_____

_____ 2 1 0

18. Consider carefully all you have learned about the store detective and the woman.

Supporting your answer by detailed reference to the text, explain whether you think the detective will have the woman charged, or let her go.

_____

_____

_____ 2 1 0

19. The story's title, "An Invisible Man", relates mainly to the store detective.
In what other way does the writer use the idea of an invisible man in the story?

_____

_____

_____ 2 1 0

[END OF QUESTION PAPER]

PAGE TOTAL

C

0860/405

NATIONAL
QUALIFICATIONS
2003

TUESDAY, 6 MAY
2.30 PM – 3.20 PM

ENGLISH
STANDARD GRADE
Credit Level
Reading
Text

Read carefully the passage overleaf. It will help if you read it twice. When you have done so, answer the questions. Use the spaces provided in the Question/Answer booklet.

SCOTTISH
QUALIFICATIONS
AUTHORITY

Scientists have at last dispelled the myth and pieced together the events that led to the extinction of this ridiculous, flightless bird

WHY THE DO

FATEFUL ENCOUNTER: The Dutch capture several of the weird birds

1   DODO. The very word conjures up an image — fat, stupid, ridiculous. Somehow we feel we know this bird. But one thing we all know is that it's dead. As dead as . . . er . . . the dodo. It's all in the name. It has that sort of childish, sing-song feel to it. Endearing because it sounds so daft. And yet the dodo is more than a cheap laugh: the dodo is an icon. It's a creature of legend, a myth like the Phoenix or the Griffin. But it's a myth that really existed. A living creature so bizarre it didn't need the human imagination to think it up — and an enigma from virtually the first moment human beings laid eyes on it a little more than 500 years ago.

2   Three hundred and fifty years later, Lewis Carroll famously caricatured the bird in *Alice in Wonderland*. He portrayed it as a pompous Victorian gentleman, complete with walking cane. With this, the dodo's journey from "real" to "surreal" was complete.

3   The story begins in Shakespeare's day. In 1598, the crew of the Dutch East Indiaman, The Amsterdam, were navigating round the Cape of Good Hope when a storm blew up and the ship was blown off course. After three weeks adrift, their battered vessel came within sight of a tropical island which they named Mauritius. They were now in the Indian Ocean and the island was a god-send. It meant they could rest and repair their boat — but most importantly it meant the half-starved crew could eat.

4   The fateful encounter now unfolded. The crew quickly came across a large bird, apparently flightless. Then, unable to evade its captors, it was quickly seized by the sailors. It was like nothing they had ever set eyes on.

5   Round in shape with a plume of tail feathers, the bird stood about three feet high, the size of an overstuffed turkey or swan. Its wings were small and useless, its head surrounded by a hood of fine feathers giving it the appearance of a monk's cowl. Yet most distinctive of all was its unfeasible-looking bill. It was huge and bulbous, possessing a businesslike hook at the end.

6   But why did the bird come to be called the dodo? It has been argued that the name reflects the bird's nonsensical appearance. Or that it sounds like the noise the bird may have made. In fact the name dodo didn't stick until other names had been tried — "Kermis" after a Dutch annual fair, then "walghvogel" which means "nauseating fowl". The name "dodo" came when the Dutch finally saw its comical side.

7   Dodomania was born. Soon Dutch artists we copying the first drawings of the bird ar including them in the fantastical "menageri‹ paintings that were all the rage. Several birds we captured and brought back to Europ‹ One found its way to London, where it wa displayed for the benefit of paying customers. B around the time Charles II had been returned the throne of England in 1660, the dodo had gon forever. What had happened to the dodo? Findir out has not been easy. Following its disappearanc all anyone had to go on were sketches an paintings. All the living specimens that had be‹ brought back to Europe were long dead. The‹ were no skeletons of the bird in museums. Rapidl the trail of the dodo began to go cold.

8   Surely this ridiculous bird, fat, flightless an vulnerable, had simply been caught and eaten extinction? Too weak or stupid to defend itself, to trusting of humans, the dodo had met its inevitab end. In a Darwinian world the dodo has con down to us as the prime example of how poorl designed and hapless creatures just won't stay the race. Sad but inevitable sums up the extinctic of the dodo. Until now. According to ornithologi Julian Hume, the fat, comical appearance of th bird is grossly exaggerated. Julian has travelled Mauritius to investigate what the bird was real‹ like and how it lived. It is here that the only tw complete skeletons of the bird exist which ha‹ proved just how misrepresented the dodo has bee‹ "Now we have the skeleton of the dodo, we can te so much more about the bird and how it may ha‹ appeared in life," says Julian. "It had a lo‹ sinuous neck, quite an upright stance, an probably stood about two and a half feet tall. Th‹ is very different from the picture that's come dow to us from those early drawings."

DO IS DEAD

FLIGHT OF FANCY: New research has shown that the dodo was not the fat, squat bird drawn by 18th century artists, rather a lean, upright creature with a powerful hooked bill

9 The dodo wasn't a fat, squat creature; it was lean and upright. Indeed, the earliest images, drawn from life, show a scrawny bird, its hooked bill making its appearance quite aggressive. The later you go, the fatter and sillier it becomes. There are many other mysteries to solve. Why was it flightless? Why did it live on Mauritius and nowhere else? How did it get there? Finding out takes us right back to the 17th century.

0 When the London dodo died, the animal was stuffed and sold to the Ashmolean Museum in Oxford. Taxidermy not being what it is today, over the next few decades the dodo slowly rotted until it was thrown out in 1755. All, that is, except the moth-eaten head and one leg.

1 Today these remnants are the only surviving dodo skin tissue in existence.

2 For more than a century scientists had assumed that the dodo's ancestors must have reached Mauritius from Africa — because this is the nearest continental land mass. In fact, Dr Shapiro has proved the dodo was south-east Asian. Its closest ancestor spent millions of years island-hopping from somewhere in the region of Burma or Indonesia until it finally arrived on Mauritius. There it stayed and, unthreatened by predators, gave up the ability to fly, massively increased in size and became the creature that the Dutch finally ran into in 1598.

13 Julian Hume believes the bird rooted at ground level, foraging fruits from palm trees and using its tough bill to break open and eat snail shells. It built its nest on the forest floor into which it had laid a single egg, possibly only every other year.

14 The dodo was master of its domain, superbly and uniquely adapted to its particular environment. Yet within 70 years of its discovery by man, it was extinct.

15 Dutch archaeologist Pieter Floore has spent several seasons excavating the rubbish dumps left by the Mauritanian Dutch colonists at Fort Hendrink, their main base. If they hunted the dodo to extinction, Floore reckoned he would be able to find evidence in the form of dodo bones among the household rubbish the Dutch threw out.

16 Yet despite several years of digging, he has not found a single dodo bone. In fact, there is no evidence whatsoever that the Dutch ever hunted and ate the dodo on any scale that would lead to its extinction.

17 Combining evidence from the skeleton and other written accounts, Julian Hume has also demonstrated that the dodo was not only quite hard to catch, but was also terrible to eat. Being flightless, it had no breast muscles and hence no breast meat. Its fat bottom was meaty but so greasy that accounts reveal that it "cloyed and nauseated the stomach" — hence the original name "walghvogel" or "nauseating fowl".

18 Yet still it perished. Just why has been revealed by archaeologist Pieter Floore. While he has never found a single dodo bone, he has uncovered tens of thousands of bones belonging to animals that the Dutch introduced to the island. Most visible are the bones of pigs, and these provide the vital clue.

19 Pigs, like dodos, are ground-rooting animals. They are easy to farm — simply release them into the forest and they will take care of themselves. As they did so they proved fatal to the dodo, disturbing ancient mating and nesting behaviour, eating the dodo's eggs, and voraciously competing for food. In Mauritius's unique island habitat, perfectly balanced for more than 10 million years, something as apparently benign as the introduction of the pig proved fatal for the dodo.

20 When a German sailor was shipwrecked on Mauritius in 1662, he walked the length and breadth of the island but saw no dodos except a few on an islet off-shore. This was the last dodo colony seen by man.

21 By 1670 the last dodo was dead and the bird had passed from reality into myth. Only now have we found the real reason why.

Adapted from an article by *Alex West*

[END OF PASSAGE]

[BLANK PAGE]

FOR OFFICIAL USE

C

Total
Mark

0860/406

NATIONAL
QUALIFICATIONS
2003

TUESDAY, 6 MAY
2.30 PM – 3.20 PM

**ENGLISH
STANDARD GRADE**
Credit Level
Reading
Questions

Fill in these boxes and read what is printed below.

Full name of centre

Town

Forename(s)

Surname

Date of birth
Day Month Year

Scottish candidate number

Number of seat

**NB Before leaving the examination room you must give this booklet to the invigilator.
If you do not, you may lose all the marks for this paper.**

SCOTTISH
QUALIFICATIONS
AUTHORITY

©

Marks

QUESTIONS

Write your answers in the spaces provided.

Look at Paragraphs 1 and 2.

1. Explain why the writer opens the passage with the single word "DODO".

   _____

   2 1

2. **According to the writer** why is the name of the dodo both familiar and memorable?

   _____

   _____

   2 1 0

3. Explain fully what is unusual about the expression "But it's a myth that really existed".

   _____

   _____

   _____

   2 1 0

4. Which **two** words does the writer use to emphasise the strangeness of the dodo?

   (i) _____

   (ii) _____

   2 1 0

5. "Lewis Carroll famously caricatured the bird"

   Explain fully how the rest of Paragraph 2 develops this idea.

   _____

   _____

   _____

   2 1 0

PAGE
TOTAL

Marks

Look at Paragraphs 3 to 6.

6. What does the writer's use of the expression "fateful encounter" tell you about the meeting?

    _____

    _____   2 ■ 0

7. "It was like nothing they had ever set eyes on."

    What is the function of this sentence?

    _____   2 ■ 0

8. In your own words, what does the writer's use of the expression "unfeasible-looking" tell you about the dodo's bill?

    _____

    _____   2 1 0

9. Explain the writer's use of a question at the beginning of Paragraph 6.

    _____

    _____   2 1 0

Look at Paragraph 7.

10. What examples of Dodomania does the writer give? Answer in your own words.

    _____

    _____

    _____   2 1 0

[Turn over

Marks

11. "Rapidly, the trail of the dodo began to go cold."

Why do you think the writer chooses to use this expression?

_____

_____   2 ■ 0

Look at Paragraphs 8 to 11.

12. Explain **in your own words** why the dodo is a good example of the theories of the "Darwinian world".

_____

_____   2 ■ 0

13. Which **one word** in Paragraph 8 sums up the writer's sympathetic attitude to the dodo?

_____   2 ■ 0

14. Give details of **two** obvious contrasts between the imagined appearance and the real appearance of the dodo.   2 1 0

(i) _____

(ii) _____

15. Why does the writer use a series of questions in Paragraph 9?

_____

_____   2 1 0

16. Explain how the context helps you to understand the meaning of "taxidermy" in Paragraph 10.

_____

_____   2 1 0

PAGE
TOTAL

Marks

Look at Paragraph 12.

17. Explain fully, **in your own words**, why the scientists "assumed" that the dodo reached Mauritius from Africa.

_____

_____

2 1 0

18. Explain fully why you think the writer chooses to use the expression "island-hopping".

_____

_____

_____

2 1 0

Look at Paragraphs 13 to 18.

19. Quote **two** expressions which suggest that Julian Hume's knowledge of the dodo is theoretical.

    (i) _____

    (ii) _____

2 1 0

20. What **two** pieces of evidence helped prove that the Dutch did not hunt the dodo to extinction?

    (i) _____

    (ii) _____

2 1 0

[Turn over for Questions 21 to 25 on *Page six*

PAGE
TOTAL

Marks

Look at Paragraphs 19 to 21.

21. **In your own words**, explain fully why the introduction of pigs proved "fatal" for the dodo.

_____

_____

_____

_____   2 1 0

22. What does the writer's use of the expression "apparently benign" tell you about the introduction of the pigs?

_____

_____   2 1 0

23. Why does the writer give the dates in the final two paragraphs?

_____

_____   2 1 0

Think about the passage as a whole.

24. The purpose of the article is to provide scientific information in a popular format. By close reference to the text, identify and comment on any technique which the writer uses to add weight to the information.

_____

_____

_____

_____   2 1 0

25. What **two key questions** are answered as a result of the information in the passage?

_____

_____

_____   2 1 0

[END OF QUESTION PAPER]

PAGE
TOTAL

C

0860/405

NATIONAL
QUALIFICATIONS
2004

WEDNESDAY, 5 MAY
2.30 PM – 3.20 PM

ENGLISH
STANDARD GRADE
Credit Level
Reading
Text

Read carefully the passage overleaf. It will help if you read it twice. When you have done so, answer the questions. Use the spaces provided in the Question/Answer booklet.

©

The following extract is taken from a novel set on a Greek island during the Second World War.

1   When Pelagia entered the kitchen she stopped singing abruptly, and was seized with consternation. There was a stranger seated at the kitchen table, a most horrible and wild stranger who looked worse than the brigands of childhood tales. The man was quite motionless except for the rhythmic fluttering and trembling of his hands. His head was utterly concealed beneath a cascade of matted hair that seemed to have no form nor colour. In places it stuck out in twisted corkscrews, and in others it lay in congealed pads like felt; it was the hair of a hermit demented by solitude. Beneath it Pelagia could see nothing but an enormous and disorderly beard surmounted by two tiny bright eyes that would not look at her. There was a nose in there, stripped of its skin, reddened and flaked, and glimpses of darkened, streaked and grimy flesh.

2   The stranger wore the unidentifiable and ragged remains of a shirt and trousers, and a kind of overcoat cut out of animal skins that had been tacked together with thongs of sinew. Pelagia saw, beneath the table, that in place of shoes his feet were bound with bandages that were both caked with old, congealed blood, and the bright stains of fresh. He was breathing heavily, and the smell was inconceivably foul; it was the reek of rotting flesh, of festering wounds, of ancient perspiration, and of fear. She looked at the hands that were clasped together in the effort to prevent their quivering, and was overcome both with fright and pity. What was she to do?

3   "My father's out," she said. "He should be back tomorrow."

4   "Ice," said the stranger, as though he had not heard her, "I'll never be warm again." His voice cracked and she realised that his shoulders were heaving. "Oh, the ice," he repeated. He held his hands before his face. He wrapped his fingers together, and his whole body seemed to be fighting to suppress a succession of spasms.

5   "You can come back tomorrow," said Pelagia, appalled by this gibbering apparition, and completely at a loss.

6   "No crampons, you see. The snow is whipped away by the wind, and the ice is in ridges, sharper than knives, and when you fall you are cut. Look at my hands." He held them up to her, palm outwards in the gesture that would normally be an insult, and she saw the horrendous cross-tracking of hard white scars that had obliterated every natural line, scored away the pads and calluses, and left seeping cracks across the joints. There were no nails and no trace of cuticles.

7   "And the ice screams. It shrieks. And voices call to you out of it. And you look into it and you see people. They beckon and wave, and they mock, and you shoot into the ice but they don't shut up, and then the ice squeaks. It squeaks all night, all night."

8   "Look, you can't stay," said Pelagia.

9   Her perplexity was growing into an acute anxiety as she wondered what on earth she was supposed to do on her own with a mad vagrant ranting in her kitchen. She thought of leaving him there and running out to fetch help; but was paralysed by the thought of what he might do or steal in her absence. "Please leave," she pleaded. "My father will be back tomorrow, and he can . . . see to your feet."

10   The man responded to her for the first time, "I can't walk. No boots."

11   Psipsina entered the room and sniffed the air, her whiskers twitching as she sampled the strong and unfamiliar smells. She ran across the floor in her fluid

manner, and leapt up onto the table. She approached the neolithic man and burrowed in the remains of a pocket, emerging triumphantly with a small cube of white cheese that she demolished with evident satisfaction. She returned to the pocket and found only a broken cigarette, which she discarded.

12   The man smiled, revealing good teeth but bleeding gums, and he petted the animal about the head. "Ah, at least Psipsina remembers me," he said, and silent tears began to follow each other down his cheeks and into his beard. "She still smells sweet."

13   Pelagia was astounded. Psipsina was afraid of strangers, and how did this ghastly ruin know her name? Who could have told him? She wiped her hands on her apron for the lack of any sense of what to think or do, and said, "Mandras?"

14   The man turned his face towards her and said, "Don't touch me, Pelagia. I've got lice. I didn't know what to do, and I came here first. All the time I knew I had to get here first, that's all, and I'm tired. Do you have any coffee?"

15   Pelagia's mind became void, decentred by a babble of emotions. She felt despair, unbearable excitement, guilt, pity, revulsion. Her heart jumped in her chest and her hands fell to her side. Perhaps more than anything else, she felt helpless. It seemed inconceivable that this desolate ghost concealed the soul and body of the man she had loved and desired and missed so much, and then finally dismissed. "You never wrote to me," she said, coming up with the first thing that entered her head, the accusation that had rankled in her mind from the moment of his departure, the accusation that had grown into an angry, resentful monster.

16   Mandras looked up wearily, and said, as though it were he that pitied her, "I can't write."

17   For a reason that she did not understand, Pelagia was more repelled by this admission than by his filth. Had she betrothed herself to an illiterate, without even knowing it? For the sake of something to say she asked, "Couldn't someone else have written for you? I thought you were dead. I thought you . . . couldn't love me."

Adapted from *Captain Corelli's Mandolin* by Louis de Bernières

[END OF PASSAGE]

[BLANK PAGE]

FOR OFFICIAL USE

C

Total
Mark

0860/406

NATIONAL
QUALIFICATIONS
2004

WEDNESDAY, 5 MAY
2.30 PM – 3.20 PM

ENGLISH
STANDARD GRADE
Credit Level
Reading
Questions

Fill in these boxes and read what is printed below.

Full name of centre

Town

Forename(s)

Surname

Date of birth
Day Month Year

Scottish candidate number

Number of seat

**NB Before leaving the examination room you must give this booklet to the invigilator.
If you do not, you may lose all the marks for this paper.**

SCOTTISH
QUALIFICATIONS
AUTHORITY

©

Marks

QUESTIONS

Write your answers in the spaces provided.

Look at Paragraph 1.

1. Quote **two** words used by the writer to convey the suddenness of Pelagia's reactions as she entered the kitchen.

    (i) _____

    (ii) _____

    2 1 0

2. Quote the expression which sums up Pelagia's impression of the stranger.

    _____

    2 ■ 0

3. **In your own words** what contrasting image does the writer give of the movements of the man?

    _____

    2 1 0

4. What **two** ideas are suggested by the expression "a hermit demented by solitude"?

    2 1 0

    (i) _____

    (ii) _____

5. Explain fully why it was difficult for Pelagia to get a clear view of the stranger's face.

    _____

    _____

    2 1 0

Look at Paragraph 2.

6. "congealed blood, and the bright stains of fresh."

    What does this description tell you about the wounds to the man's feet?

    _____

    2 1 0

PAGE
TOTAL

Marks

7. "it was the reek of rotting flesh . . . fear."

Explain fully how the writer emphasises the smell from the stranger

  (i) through sentence structure.

_____

_____ 2 1 0

  (ii) through word choice.

_____

_____ 2 1 0

8. (a) **In your own words** what **two** conflicting emotions did Pelagia feel when she looked at the man?

_____ 2 1 0

  (b) Explain how the writer conveys Pelagia's dilemma.

_____ 2 ■ 0

Look at Paragraphs 3 to 5.

9. "My father's out," she said. "He should be back tomorrow."

What does Pelagia hope to achieve by making this statement?

_____ 2 ■ 0

10. Why is "gibbering" (Paragraph 5) an appropriate word to describe the stranger at this point?

_____

_____ 2 1 0

[Turn over

PAGE
TOTAL

Marks

Look at Paragraphs 6 and 7.

11. What **two** features of the ice disturbed the man most?

    (i) _____

    (ii) _____

2 1

12. **Identify** any **two techniques** used by the writer in Paragraph 7 which help to convey the man's sense of panic and distress.

    (i) _____

    (ii) _____

2 1

Look at Paragraphs 8 to 10.

13. What are the options that Pelagia is considering in Paragraph 9?

    _____

    _____

2 1 0

Look at Paragraphs 11 and 12.

14. Quote **two** words from Paragraph 11 which suggest that Psipsina was unhappy with her second visit to the man's pocket.

    (i) _____

    (ii) _____

2 1 0

15. "Ah, at least Psipsina remembers me," (Paragraph 12)

    What does this imply about the man's feelings towards Pelagia?

    _____

2 ■ 0

PAGE
TOTAL

Marks

Look at Paragraphs 13 and 14.

16. "Pelagia was astounded."

    How does the sentence structure in the rest of this paragraph develop Pelagia's sense of astonishment?

    _____

    _____   2 1 0

17. "The man turned his face towards her and said, 'Don't touch me, Pelagia.'"

    Why might this statement by Mandras be considered ironic?

    _____

    _____   2 1 0

Look at Paragraphs 15 to 17.

18. Tick (✓) the appropriate box to show which of the following best describes the relationship between Mandras and Pelagia.

    Brother ☐   Father ☐

    Husband ☐   Fiancé ☐

    Justify your answer with close reference to the text.

    _____

    _____   2 1 0

19. **Identify one way** in which the writer conveys the intensity of Pelagia's feelings about the fact that Mandras had not written.

    _____

    _____   2 ■ 0

[Turn over for Questions 20 to 22 on *Page six*

PAGE
TOTAL

Marks

20. **In your own words** explain fully how Pelagia felt when Mandras confessed he could not write.

_____

_____   2 1 0

Think about the passage as a whole.

21. How does each of the characters change in the course of the passage? **(Clear change must be indicated.)**

Pelagia _____

_____

_____   2 1 0

Mandras _____

_____

_____   2 1 0

22. For whom do you feel more sympathy – Pelagia or Mandras?

Justify your choice by close reference to the passage.

_____

_____

_____   2 1 0

[*END OF QUESTION PAPER*]

PAGE TOTAL

2002 FOUNDATION, GENERAL AND CREDIT

FGC

0860/407

NATIONAL
QUALIFICATIONS
2002

TUESDAY, 7 MAY
9.00 AM – 10.15 AM

ENGLISH
STANDARD GRADE
Foundation, General
and Credit Levels
Writing

Read This First

1   Inside this booklet, there are photographs and words.
    Use them to help you when you are thinking about what to write.
    Look at all the material and think about all the possibilities.

2   There are 23 assignments altogether for you to choose from.

3   Decide which assignment you are going to attempt.
    Choose only **one** and write its number in the margin of your answer book.

4   Pay close attention to what you are asked to write.
    Plan what you are going to write.
    Read and check your work before you hand it in.
    Any changes to your work should be made clearly.

SCOTTISH
QUALIFICATIONS
AUTHORITY

MCB 0860/407 6/70170   ©

FIRST   **Look at the picture opposite.**
               It shows a cat, a dog and a mouse in an awkward situation.

NEXT   Think about possible conflicts.

WHAT YOU HAVE TO WRITE

1. **Write about** a time when you were in conflict with someone over a particular issue.

   Be sure to include your thoughts and feelings.

   OR

2. "Don't blame the animals; blame their owners."
   Discuss.

   OR

3. **Write in any way you wish** using **one** of the following titles:

        No Escape   Unlikely Friends

[Turn over

FIRST   **Look at the picture opposite.**
         It shows something left behind or forgotten.

NEXT   Think about the ideas of loss and surprise.

WHAT YOU HAVE TO WRITE

4. **Write about** a time when you lost something special, making clear how you felt and why.

   OR

5. **Imagine** that you are the person on the train. Your music case has just been left on the platform. **Write the story.**

   OR

6. "The young people of today have no sense of value."
   What do you think? **Give your views.**

   OR

7. **Write a short story** using **one** of the following titles:

   Too late   Life is Full of Surprises

[Turn over

FIRST   **Look at the picture opposite.
It shows a successful athlete.**

NEXT   Think about personal achievement and the impact of sport.

WHAT YOU HAVE TO WRITE

8. **Write about** a time when you experienced personal success and achievement, concentrating on your thoughts and feelings.

   OR

9. Designer sports gear—nothing more than a fashion statement? A waste of money?
   Discuss.

   OR

10. "A healthier generation should be encouraged through school sports.
    Discuss.

    OR

11. **Write a newspaper report** with the title:
    Winner Takes All

                                                                [Turn over

Page eight

FIRST   **Look at the picture opposite.**
                  It shows an icebound ship.

NEXT   Think about the risk taking, endurance and survival.

WHAT YOU HAVE TO WRITE
---

12. Write a detailed entry for **one day** which might appear in the journal of a crew member on this ship.

    OR

13. "I will survive."

    Write about your thoughts and feelings at a time in your life when you feel that you endured and survived.

    OR

14. Are we developing into a nation of irresponsible risk takers?
    Discuss.

    OR

15. **Write in any way you wish** using **one** of the following titles:

    The Survivor   Waiting For . . .

[Turn over

FIRST **Look at the picture opposite.
It shows a nuclear power station.**

NEXT Think about different kinds of power.

WHAT YOU HAVE TO WRITE

16. "To save our planet we must look for alternative sources of power."

    Do you agree or disagree? **Give your views**.

    OR

17. **Describe a visit** you have made to **a place of work** which made a lasting impression on you. In your description be sure to include not only the place but also your thoughts and feelings.

    OR

18. **Write about** a time when you were given a certain amount of power or responsibility and used it wisely or unwisely.

    OR

19. **Write in any way you wish** using **one** of the following titles:

    Meltdown   Chain Reaction   Fallout

    [Turn over for assignments 20 to 23 on *Page twelve*

There are no pictures for these assignments.

20. Choose **one** of the following and continue the story:

The map and instructions had been quite clear and he had faithfully followed them. Yet, here he sat not knowing what road to take and what the next step of the journey would hold.

OR

She had waited and then waited again so many times but her moment had never come. Now she had her chance to make the difference.

OR

21. "The days of chalk and talk have gone and have been replaced by learning through new information technology systems."

Agree or disagree.

OR

22. **Describe the scene** suggested by **one** of the following:

The sea is calm tonight
The tide is full, the moon lies fair
Upon the Straits

Matthew Arnold

OR

The fair breeze blew, the white foam flew,
The furrow followed free;
We were the first that ever burst
Into that silent sea.

Coleridge

OR

23. Write a tale of mystery and imagination.

[END OF QUESTION PAPER]

2003 FOUNDATION, GENERAL AND CREDIT

F
G
C

0860/407

NATIONAL QUALIFICATIONS 2003

TUESDAY, 6 MAY 9.00 AM – 10.15 AM

ENGLISH
STANDARD GRADE
Foundation, General
and Credit Levels
Writing

Read This First

1 Inside this booklet, there are photographs and words.
Use them to help you when you are thinking about what to write.
Look at all the material and think about all the possibilities.

2 There are 22 assignments altogether for you to choose from.

3 Decide which assignment you are going to attempt.
Choose only **one** and write its number in the margin of your answer book.

4 Pay close attention to what you are asked to write.
Plan what you are going to write.
Read and check your work before you hand it in.
Any changes to your work should be made clearly.

SCOTTISH
QUALIFICATIONS
AUTHORITY

SAB 0860/407 6/71570

©

FIRST   **Look at the picture opposite.**
                 It shows someone walking across a bridge into the fog.

NEXT   Think about a place with an eerie, mysterious atmosphere.

WHAT YOU HAVE TO WRITE

1. **Write a story** using the following opening.

   Jan squared her shoulders and steeled herself against the biting cold. Staring ahead intently, she strode off into the chill fog . . .

   OR

2. Sometimes in darkest winter, all we want to do is huddle up in front of the fire and . . .

   Write about a special memory of such an occasion.

   You should include your **thoughts and feelings.**

   OR

3. **Write in any way you choose** using the picture opposite as your inspiration.

   OR

4. **Write a short story** using **ONE** of the following titles:

   The Stranger   The Fog   Into the Darkness

[Turn over

FIRST   **Look at the picture opposite.**
          It shows a spider's web.

NEXT   Think about feeling trapped or being in danger.

> WHAT YOU HAVE TO WRITE

5. **Write about an incident** in your life when you felt that there was no escape.

   Remember to include your **thoughts and feelings.**

   OR

6. **Write in any way you choose** using **ONE** of the following titles:

   The Web   Trapped   The Net

   OR

7. The natural world is in danger if we do not take steps to protect it. **Write your views.**

[Turn over

FIRST **Look at the picture opposite.**
It shows a picture of a fantasy hero.

NEXT Think about action heroes/heroines.

WHAT YOU HAVE TO WRITE
---

8. Fantasy heroes/heroines make good role models for the young.

   Write your views.

   OR

9. Write about a time when you felt that your actions were heroic. Remember to include your **thoughts and feelings.**

   OR

10. Violence on the screen encourages violence in real life.

    Discuss.

    OR

11. **Write a short story** using the title:

    The Warrior.

[Turn over

FIRST **Look at the picture opposite.**
It shows a CCTV camera sign.

NEXT Think about your privacy.

WHAT YOU HAVE TO WRITE

12. CCTV cameras and curfews are effective but unpopular methods of cutting crime.

    Discuss.

    OR

13. Write about an occasion in your life when you were caught doing something wrong.

    Remember to include your **thoughts and feelings.**

    OR

14. **Write a short story** using the following title:

    Caught on Camera.

[Turn over

FIRST **Look at the picture opposite.**
It shows a wave crashing against a sea wall.

NEXT Think about the power of nature.

WHAT YOU HAVE TO WRITE

---

15. Write about a time when you were caught in bad weather.

You should include your **thoughts and feelings.**

OR

16. Winters get windier; summers get wetter.

Write about your views on our changing climate.

OR

17. **Write a short story** using **ONE** of the following titles:

The Storm   The Force

OR

18. Storm Damage Widespread.

Write a newspaper report using this headline.

[Turn over for assignments 19 to 22 on *Page twelve*

There are no pictures for these assignments.

Describe the scene brought to mind by **ONE** of the following:

19. "A ship is floating in the harbour now,

A wind is hovering o'er the mountain's brow . . ."

P B Shelley

OR

"The woods are lovely, dark and deep . . ."

Robert Frost

OR

"All shod with steel

We hissed along the polished ice . . ."

William Wordsworth

OR

20. My Ideal Webpage.

What features would you include in your ideal webpage and why?

OR

21. Today we have too many rights and not enough responsibilities.

Do you agree or disagree?

Write your views.

OR

22. Write a short story entitled:

The Attic.

[END OF QUESTION PAPER]

2004 FOUNDATION, GENERAL AND CREDIT

F G C

0860/407

| NATIONAL QUALIFICATIONS 2004 | WEDNESDAY, 5 MAY 9.00 AM – 10.15 AM | ENGLISH STANDARD GRADE Foundation, General and Credit Levels Writing |

Read This First

1   Inside this booklet, there are photographs and words.
    Use them to help you when you are thinking about what to write.
    Look at all the material and think about all the possibilities.

2   There are 22 assignments altogether for you to choose from.

3   Decide which assignment you are going to attempt.
    Choose only **one** and write its number in the margin of your answer book.

4   Pay close attention to what you are asked to write.
    Plan what you are going to write.
    Read and check your work before you hand it in.
    Any changes to your work should be made clearly.

SCOTTISH
QUALIFICATIONS
AUTHORITY

©

FIRST **Look at the picture opposite.**
It shows a picture of a communications satellite.

NEXT Think about the advantages and disadvantages of communications technology.

WHAT YOU HAVE TO WRITE

1. The more television channels there are, the harder it is to find something good to watch.

   Do you agree or disagree?

   Give your views.

   OR

2. **Write a short story** in which a mobile phone plays an important part.

   OR

3. The Internet continues to make the world smaller.

   Write about the **advantages and disadvantages** of the Internet.

[Turn over

Page four

FIRST **Look at the pictures opposite.**
       They show a young woman staring over mountain peaks,
       and a city scene.

NEXT   Think about special places you have visited.

WHAT YOU HAVE TO WRITE

4. **Write about** whether you would prefer to live in the city or the country.

   Give reasons for your choice.

   OR

5. **Write in any way you choose** using **one or both** of the pictures as your inspiration.

   OR

6. A view I will always remember.

   Write about a place which had this effect on you.

   OR

7. **Write a short story** with the title:

   No Time to Spare

   [Turn over

FIRST   **Look at the picture opposite.**
         It shows a student looking through the hub of a wheel.

NEXT   Think about the world of work.

WHAT YOU HAVE TO WRITE

8. **Write an informative article** for your school magazine on a career which you want to follow when you leave school.

   OR

9. In our everyday lives we depend too much on machines.

   Discuss.

   OR

10. **Write a letter** to a local newspaper putting the case for more education for work.

    OR

11. **Write about** an occasion in your life when teamwork was vital.

    Remember to include your **thoughts and feelings.**

[Turn over

Page eight

FIRST **Look at the picture opposite.
It shows a young boy winning a race.**

NEXT Think about what it feels like to take part in an event.

WHAT YOU HAVE TO WRITE

12. **Write about** an achievement you remember above all others.

    Remember to include your **thoughts and feelings.**

    OR

13. Communities today do not have enough organised events to suit young people.

    Discuss.

    OR

14. "It is the taking part that is important, not the winning."

    Do you agree or disagree?

    Give your views.

    OR

15. **Write a short story** using the title:

    Crossing The Line

    [Turn over

FIRST   **Look at the picture opposite.**
It shows a man looking out of his house window over a city.

NEXT   Think about what it feels like to be different.

WHAT YOU HAVE TO WRITE

---

16. **Write a short story** about a character who is isolated from society.

    OR

17. **Write in any way you choose** using **one** of the following titles:

    Keeper of the City   Success   The Glass House

    OR

18. **Write a description** of your ideal home.

    OR

19. Even famous people have a right to privacy.

    Do you agree or disagree?

    Give your views.

[Turn over for assignments 20 to 22 on *Page twelve*

There are no pictures for these assignments.

20. "Shop till you drop."

    Retail therapy does more harm than good.
    Discuss.

    OR

21. **Describe the scene** brought to mind by **one** of the following:

    For winter rains and ruins are over,
    And all the season of snows

    Swinburne

    OR

    He will watch from dawn to gloom
    The lake-reflected sun

    Shelley

    OR

    The rocky summits, split and rent,
    Formed turret, dome, or battlement

    Scott

22. **Write a short story** using the title:

    Appearances Can Be Deceptive

[END OF QUESTION PAPER]

[BLANK PAGE]

[BLANK PAGE]